AF677300

Scotiabank Group®

Dear Reader:

Scotiabank is pleased to make this important book available, simplifying the benefits of the new Tax-Free Savings Account (TFSA). We hope you find the savings strategies and best practices helpful in making the most of what you have.

As Gordon Pape demonstrates in this book, a TFSA can be an important part of your overall investment strategy. Read on and see why many Canadians feel that Scotiabank's TFSA is a savings opportunity that's worth having. We also encourage you to see for yourself how quickly your tax savings and TFSA balance can grow by using Scotiabank's TFSA Calculator at scotiabank.com/tfsatool.

If you have any doubts or questions about how you are invested, I invite you to get a Second Opinion from any advisor of the Scotiabank Group. It's free, confidential, and no obligation. And it's a great way to explore your options. Because with savings options like these, you're richer than you think.

Enjoy the book,

Barbara Mason
EVP, Wealth Management Canada
Scotiabank Group

PENGUIN CANADA

TAX-FREE SAVINGS ACCOUNTS

GORDON PAPE is Canada's best known financial author and the publisher of five investment newsletters, including *The Income Investor, Mutual Funds Update, The Canada Report*, and *The Internet Wealth Builder*. He is the author of several national bestsellers, including *Sleep-Easy Investing* and *The Retirement Time Bomb*, and has spoken at hundreds of seminars in Canada and the United States. Pape is frequently quoted in the media and is a popular guest on radio and television shows. His website is located at www.BuildingWealth.ca.

Also by Gordon Pape

INVESTMENT ADVICE

Sleep-Easy Investing

The Retirement Time Bomb

Get Control of Your Money

6 Steps to $1 Million

Retiring Wealthy in the 21st Century

The Complete Guide to RRIFs and LIFs (with David Tafler)

Gordon Pape's 2004 Buyer's Guide to Mutual Funds (with Eric Kirzner)

Gordon Pape's 2004 Buyer's Guide to RRSPs

Secrets of Successful Investing (with Eric Kirzner)

Gordon Pape's Investing Strategies 2001 (with Richard Croft and Eric Kirzner)

Making Money in Mutual Funds

The Canadian Mortgage Book (with Bruce McDougall)

The Best of Pape's Notes

Head Start (with Frank Jones)

Retiring Wealthy

Building Wealth in the '90s

Low-Risk Investing in the '90s

Low-Risk Investing

Building Wealth

CONSUMER ADVICE

Gordon Pape's International Shopping Guide (with Deborah Kerbel)

HUMOUR

The $50,000 Stove Handle

CHRISTMAS (with Deborah Kerbel)

Quizmas Carols

Family Quizmas

Quizmas: Christmas Trivia Family Fun (www.quizmas.net)

FICTION (with Tony Aspler)

Chain Reaction

The Scorpion Sanction

The Music Wars

NON-FICTION

Montreal at the Crossroads (with Donna Gabeline and Dane Lanken)

TAX-FREE SAVINGS ACCOUNTS

A Guide to TFSAs and How They Can Make You Rich

Gordon Pape

PENGUIN
CANADA

PENGUIN CANADA

Published by the Penguin Group

Penguin Group (Canada), 90 Eglinton Avenue East, Suite 700,
Toronto, Ontario, Canada M4P 2Y3 (a division of Pearson Canada Inc.)

Penguin Group (USA) Inc., 375 Hudson Street, New York, New York 10014, U.S.A.
Penguin Books Ltd, 80 Strand, London WC2R 0RL, England
Penguin Ireland, 25 St Stephen's Green, Dublin 2, Ireland (a division of Penguin Books Ltd)
Penguin Group (Australia), 250 Camberwell Road, Camberwell, Victoria 3124, Australia
(a division of Pearson Australia Group Pty Ltd)
Penguin Books India Pvt Ltd, 11 Community Centre, Panchsheel Park,
New Delhi – 110 017, India
Penguin Group (NZ), 67 Apollo Drive, Rosedale, North Shore 0632, New Zealand
(a division of Pearson New Zealand Ltd)
Penguin Books (South Africa) (Pty) Ltd, 24 Sturdee Avenue, Rosebank,
Johannesburg 2196, South Africa

Penguin Books Ltd, Registered Offices: 80 Strand, London WC2R 0RL, England

First published 2009

1 2 3 4 5 6 7 8 9 10 (WEB)

Copyright © Gordon Pape Enterprises Ltd., 2009

All rights reserved. Without limiting the rights under copyright reserved above,
no part of this publication may be reproduced, stored in or introduced into a retrieval system,
or transmitted in any form or by any means (electronic, mechanical, photocopying,
recording or otherwise), without the prior written permission of both the copyright owner
and the above publisher of this book.

This publication contains the opinions and ideas of its author and is designed to provide useful advice in regard to the subject matter covered. The author and publisher are not engaged in rendering legal, accounting, or other professional services in this publication. This publication is not intended to provide a basis for action in particular circumstances without consideration by a competent professional. The author and publisher expressly disclaim any responsibility for any liability, loss, or risk, personal or otherwise, which is incurred as a consequence, directly or indirectly, of the use and application of any of the contents of this book.

Manufactured in Canada.

Library and Archives Canada Cataloguing in Publication data
available upon request to the publisher.

ISBN: 978-0-14-317239-0

Visit the Penguin Group (Canada) website at **www.penguin.ca**

Special and corporate bulk purchase rates available; please see
www.penguin.ca/corporatesales or call 1-800-810-3104, ext. 477 or 474

To the memory of Shirley Peterson—one of the warmest, kindest, most gracious ladies my wife and I have ever had the privilege to know. She is greatly missed by all those who were touched by her remarkable life.

—Gordon and Shirley Pape

Contents

Introduction

When I finished writing *Sleep-Easy Investing* in the summer of 2007, I sincerely believed it would be my last financial book.

Over a 20-year span, starting with *Building Wealth* in 1987, I authored or co-authored more than 40 books on investing and personal finance, including annual guides to mutual funds and Registered Retirement Savings Plans (RRSPs) from 1990 to 2004. Frankly, I was tired. Even more important, I felt there was nothing more I could usefully contribute.

That's why in the acknowledgments to *Sleep-Easy Investing* I thanked all my faithful readers over the years and said goodbye. Fortunately, I took a cue from J.K. Rowling and left the door open just a crack.

So here I am, barely 18 months later, with yet another book. What changed?

Tax-Free Savings Accounts are what changed. In the summer of 2007, few people seriously expected we would see such a radical transformation of the Canadian investment landscape from the Conservative government. When Finance Minister Jim Flaherty introduced the program in his 2008 Budget Speech, he handed the Canadian people the most powerful wealth-creating opportunity since the introduction of RRSPs by John Diefenbaker half a century ago.

Unfortunately, these new plans have been burdened with the awkward acronym of TFSA, which I have taken to pronouncing as "tifsa" for purposes of verbal shorthand. Whether the pronunciation catches on is immaterial, of course. No one can formulate a word from RRSP, but just look at how important it has become in our investment universe.

There's no doubt in my mind that a decade from now, Canadians will have socked away hundreds of millions of dollars in TFSA plans. Finance ministers in future cash-strapped governments may find themselves wondering whatever possessed the Conservatives to introduce a program that enabled people to shelter so much money from the Canada Revenue Agency—not just for many years, as with RRSPs, but forever!

In fact, the time may come when TFSAs surpass RRSPs in total assets, although that would take a few decades.

These accounts enable every Canadian to reduce his or her lifetime tax bill by many thousands of dollars. Younger people will be the biggest beneficiaries, and Finance Minister Jim Flaherty told the Montreal meeting of the International Economic Forum of the Americas in June 2008 that the brightest of them had already figured that out.

"I was at one of our universities the other day and the business students, 18, 19, 20 years old, they know all about this plan," he said. "And they've looked at it, the miracle of compound interest—Warren Buffett would love this—of what it means over time in terms of accrual of tax-free savings."

Flaherty estimates that within 15 to 20 years, about 90 percent of our personal savings will be held in tax-sheltered accounts such as TFSAs, RRSPs, and RRIFs. Think about that: 90 percent of our wealth will be tax-sheltered, and a large amount of that will be in TFSAs.

In September 2008, I gave a seminar on pension planning in Toronto. During the course of the discussion, I mentioned the new Tax-Free Savings Accounts, which were due to come into effect less than four months later, on January 1, 2009. I immediately sensed that no one seemed to know what I was talking about. When I asked how many of the participants were familiar with TFSAs, not a single hand was raised. I was astonished.

So I asked my children what they knew about the program. The reaction was the same. I put the question to friends and acquaintances, many of whom are financially savvy. A few were familiar with the concept but didn't know the details. A survey conducted by Scotiabank during the spring of 2008 confirmed my anecdotal observations. It found that public awareness of the program was extremely limited at that time, with only 37 percent of respondents having heard at least "a little" about it and 40 percent saying they were completely unaware of the plan.

That's when I decided that my retirement from book writing was over. We were months away from the introduction of an incredibly powerful savings engine, yet hardly anyone in Canada seemed to know about it or to have planned for it.

This book intends to change that. My goal is to provide you with all the facts you need to make the most effective use of this new tax-savings program and to provide guidance for how best to use TFSAs as you deal with the many financial decisions you will face in the coming years.

Believe me, TFSAs can make you rich! Don't pass up the opportunity.

1

The Launch: Budget 2008

No one expected much when Finance Minister Jim Flaherty stood up to give his Budget Speech in the House of Commons at 4 P.M. on February 26, 2008.

The cupboard was pretty much bare. The Conservative government, anticipating an early election, had dipped deeply into the nation's dwindling surplus the previous October, when Flaherty had delivered an Economic Statement that was actually a mini-budget in very thin disguise.

At that time, the finance minister had announced a second cut in the Goods and Services Tax (GST), reducing it to 5 percent, as the Tories had promised during their election campaign. He had announced a reduction of half a percentage point in the lowest tier income tax rate. He had increased personal tax exemptions across the board for all Canadians. He had cut the rates on Employment Insurance. He had announced deep cuts to the federal corporate tax rate, slashing it from 22.1 percent to 15 percent by 2012.

The total cost of all those tax goodies was estimated at a whopping $188.1 billion over the next six fiscal years. Of that,

$72.7 billion was eaten up by the GST cut, $64.9 billion went to income tax savings, and $50.5 billion to the corporate tax cuts.

But after handing out all those goodies, the Conservatives discovered the opposition parties were in no mood to force an election. Instead, they went along with every measure presented to them by the government, thwarting Stephen Harper's plans for an early election.

That left the government with no choice but to bring in a new budget. No one expected much. In the days leading up to the speech, the media talked about green initiatives, municipal infrastructure, more aid to students, and minor tinkering with the GST. Yawners all!

So when Flaherty rose to speak, expectations were low and the public was largely uninterested. He attempted to change that right off the top.

"Mr. Speaker," he intoned in the usual formality of the House of Commons, "the budget is balanced. Taxes have been cut. And Canadians will now have a powerful new incentive to save money, tax-free: the Tax-Free Savings Account that we are announcing today."[1]

Tax-Free Savings Accounts (TFSAs), which no one had previously thought much about, were suddenly centre stage in the most important parliamentary event of the year.

From there, the minister droned on about the strength of the Canadian economy and all the great things the Conservatives had done for taxpayers since taking office in February 2006. He was about one-third of the way through the Budget Speech when he returned to the only major new initiative he had to offer.

"If we are to help families prepare for the long term, we must ensure Canadians have the right incentives to save for the future," he said. "Saving isn't always easy. But it's important.

Unfortunately, for too long, government punished people who did the right thing.

"As one of my constituents recently said to me: 'I go to work. I collect my pay. I pay my taxes. And after I pay my expenses each month, I try to put some money away. I don't have a lot. But I am reaching my goal.

"'Yet, the federal government taxes me on what I earn on my savings and my investments. Savings and investments I socked away with after-tax income. Why am I being punished for doing the right thing?'

"Mr. Speaker, he's right. And we're going to change that.

"The Government will unveil the single most important personal savings vehicle since the introduction of the RRSP: the Tax-Free Savings Account. This flexible, registered, general-purpose account will allow Canadians to watch their savings grow, tax-free.

"It's the first account of its kind in Canadian history."

Flaherty offered a few examples of how the new program would benefit ordinary Canadians. It will, he suggested, help young people save for their first car or their first home. It will help seniors "stretch their retirement savings further."

In fact, TFSAs will allow "every Canadian to set aside a bit of cash each month for a special project, to help their kids, or to simply treat themselves."[2]

Best of all, the program will not cost much, at least initially. In the accompanying Budget Papers, the Department of Finance estimated that TFSAs will cost Ottawa only $5 million in lost revenue in the 2008–2009 fiscal year—a mere pittance.

The program will gradually become more expensive over time: $50 million in forgone revenue in 2009–2010, rising to $385 million by 2012–2013. But that is still just a drop in the bucket for a government that collects more than $240 billion in annual revenue.

Eventually, some 20 years down the road, TFSAs will cost Ottawa an estimated $3 billion annually. But that will be a problem for some future finance minister to deal with.

First reactions to the new savings plan were tepid for the most part. Media reports tended to focus on the economic aspects of the budget and on the comment by Liberal leader Stéphane Dion that his party might vote against it and bring down the government. (He quickly backed off that position.)

The *National Post* was one of the few newspapers to highlight the TFSA program, calling it "the major budget surprise." However, the *Post* commented that it was "only one of a grab bag of relatively inexpensive goodies."

Jeff Rubin, chief economist of CIBC World Markets, said that making TFSAs the star attraction of the budget was "bizarre." He told the *Post*: "It was really trivial. They are forecasting a $50-million tax expenditure next year for three-and-a-half million taxpayers. It works out to $14 per person … [that] doesn't seem to me to be what the centre piece of a budget should be. You have to have something sexy in there."[3]

(Seven months later, CIBC published a report that predicted TFSAs would generate $20 billion worth of business for Bay Street in 2009 and $115 billion in five years.[4])

Over at *The Globe and Mail*, writer Steven Chase suggested that Tax-Free Savings Accounts were "the Tories' attempt to make up for the fact they have not delivered on a poorly drafted 2006 election promise for a tax break on capital gains that would have immediately cost Ottawa billions of dollars annually."[5]

Rob Carrick, personal finance columnist for *The Globe and Mail*, was more enthusiastic, writing: "If the government gets this budget passed, TFSAs will become ubiquitous in a few years. Even though the tax savings aren't dramatic, most households will have at least a few of these plans. The TFSA is the sort of measure you rarely see introduced."[6]

Of course, the budget did pass through Parliament, the regulations were put into place, and now TFSAs are part of our investment options. Most Canadians completely forgot about them in the 10 months between announcement and implementation, but now they're here and it's time to start reaping the benefits of this unique program.

2

A Little History

The idea of the Tax-Free Savings Account did not spring fully formed from the mind of Finance Minister Jim Flaherty. In fact, his predecessor, Liberal Finance Minister Ralph Goodale, had raised the issue in both his 2003 and 2004 budgets with a promise that it would be studied.

In the 2003 budget, the government said it would "examine and consult" on whether what were at the time called Tax-Prepaid Savings Plans (TPSPs) might be "a useful and appropriate additional savings vehicle for Canadians."

In Annex 9 of the 2004 Budget Plan, the government gave the impression that the idea was moving up on the priority list. The document stated:

> Finance officials consulted with interested groups, experts and academics on the tax treatment of savings and TPSPs. The discussions were helpful in gathering views on how the tax treatment of savings could be improved and on TPSPs in particular. The Department is reviewing the views brought forward and is continuing to examine and assess TPSPs and other approaches to improve the tax treatment of savings. In

> the consultation, the question of whether a new type of savings plan such as a TPSP could be appropriate for Canada raised a number of important issues which require further consideration.[1]

But there was no reference to the plan in Goodale's 2005 budget (his final one, as it turned out). At the time, an official with the Department of Finance told me that after a meeting between senior officials and unnamed experts, it had been decided to shelve the program and simply raise RRSP contribution limits instead.

The reasons for abandoning the concept at that time were never clearly spelled out. However, those familiar with the discussions believe that officials in Finance were concerned about two issues: the cost of such a program over time and the potential political fallout when Guaranteed Income Supplement (GIS) recipients with RRSPs or Registered Retirement Income Funds (RRIFs) caught on to the fact that their benefits were being clawed back as they drew out money while people with TFSAs were not being similarly penalized. As well, there had been growing complaints over the years about the complexity of the tax system, and introducing TFSAs would add another dimension to that problem.

Another factor was the absence of any strong voter constituency to support the idea. The social rationale for the TFSA concept is that it will be of the greatest benefit to people with modest incomes. But they don't have the kind of political clout that, for example, farmers and manufacturers do.

So the TPSP concept remained in limbo for four years, until Jim Flaherty suddenly, and unexpectedly, resurrected it as TFSA in the 2008 budget.

As I noted in Chapter 1, there had been no hint it was coming. Pre-budget speculation took a "cupboard is bare" stance, noting that the finance minister had trotted out all his goodies in the previous fall's Economic Statement, which at the time was expected to kick off an election campaign. However, the opposition parties refused to co-operate in that scheme by defeating the Conservatives in the House of Commons, leaving Flaherty with nothing more to give.

The minister went out of his way to dampen budget expectations, saying in advance that he was not going to "throw money around" or put the country back into deficit by cutting taxes further.

"The fiscal chickens have come home, and are roosting uneasily on Jim Flaherty's shoulders," *The Globe and Mail* commented in a pre-budget editorial. "His options are far narrower now. His leeway is lost. The GST was the wrong tax to cut, at the wrong time. Now Mr. Flaherty has to pinch pennies."[2]

Faced with the prospect of a ho-hum budget in what would likely be an election year (and was, as it turned out), the finance minister and his staff started casting around for ideas. In pre-budget consultations with a range of business people, academics, and special interest groups, Finance officials kept returning to two key themes: demographics and retirement. As a subtext, the minister was very aware of the lingering anger among many seniors over his decision to impose a tax on income trusts, which was announced October 31, 2006.

In its "shadow budget" brief to the government prior to the 2008 budget, the C.D. Howe Institute returned to the theme of Tax-Free Savings Accounts, which it had been promoting since 2001 (more on that in a moment). However, it rated only six lines in a 13-page report—it was almost as if the institute had given up.[3]

Whether it was that reference or something else that was the trigger, the minister seized on the idea. It was a good ideological fit:

The concept had been part of his party's 2004 campaign platform (a campaign the Tories lost to Paul Martin's Liberals). On page 16 of the platform, a one-line sentence in the tax section had made this promise: "Introduce a new Registered Lifetime Savings Plan that will allow Canadians to withdraw their money tax-free."[4]

Interestingly, the concept was not restated in the 2006 platform, *Stand Up for Canada*. Instead, the Tories promised a much more sweeping overhaul of investment policy, saying they would "eliminate the capital gains tax for individuals on the sale of assets when the proceeds are reinvested within six months." Expanding on this, the platform went on: "Canadians who invest, or inherit cottages or family heirlooms, should be able to sell those assets and plough their profits back into the economy without taking a tax hit. It is time government rewarded Canadians who reinvest their money and create jobs." When I visited the official website of the Conservative Party in September 2008, while the election campaign was on, the 2006 platform had been expunged. A Google search enabled me to retrieve it from www.scribd.com.[5]

The 2004 campaign promise was clearly based on the same concept that Goodale had mused about in his 2003 and 2004 budgets, which is perhaps why the Conservatives chose to abandon it in 2006. But by early winter 2008, things were looking desperate, and Flaherty needed a showcase idea that wouldn't cost much but that would have broad appeal and look good in the media headlines. The TFSA concept fit the bill—especially the negligible initial cost. It also had the added attraction of addressing the 2006 capital gains promise, albeit on a much scaled-back basis. The minister had his officials massage it into a comprehensive plan and took it to Prime Minister Harper, who micro-manages everything in Ottawa these days. Once Harper signed on, Cabinet approval was virtually a rubber stamp. Months later, during the

2008 election campaign, Harper described TFSAs as "our first cut" at capital gains tax reform during an interview with Amanda Lang of Business News Network.

So both the Liberals and the Conservatives looked at the TFSA concept between 2003 and 2005, although it was never presented as a high priority. But where did the original idea come from?

The British Model

Great Britain created a similar program a decade ago, in April 1999. The Individual Savings Account (ISA) has become quite popular. According to a report written by CIBC senior economist Benjamin Tal in September 2008, 37 percent of British citizens have opened ISAs, contributing an average of £2500 a year (the maximum allowed is £7200). Tal said the number of new accounts is increasing at an annual rate of 6 percent and that ISAs have become a £270 billion market in the United Kingdom.

The Canadian TFSA concept is closely modelled on the British program but offers more flexibility to investors. The British plan imposes restrictions on what people can invest in, requiring that at least 50 percent of the money be held in cash. Under amendments introduced in 2007, ISA holders can invest up to £3600 a year in a cash plan and another £3600 in what is called a stocks and shares ISA. Obviously, this limit reduces the growth potential of the program.[6]

Offsetting that is the much higher annual contribution limit in the United Kingdom. Using an exchange rate of £1 equals CDN$1.90, U.K. residents can contribute the equivalent of CDN$13,680 a year to an ISA, almost triple the initial contribution limit in this country.

The Roth IRA

In the United States, the closest thing to the ISA or the TFSA is the Roth Individual Retirement Account (Roth IRA). It actually predates the ISA, having been created in 1998, but it is nowhere near as attractive a savings vehicle as the other two.

As with the British and Canadian plans, contributions to a Roth IRA are not tax-deductible. Unlike the others, however, the maximum annual amount that can be contributed is determined by age. In 2008, Americans under age 50 were allowed to contribute a maximum of $5000 a year, while older citizens could contribute up to $6000. Income earned by investments in a Roth IRA are tax-sheltered but can only be withdrawn from the plan tax-free after a holding period of five years or when the investor reaches the age of 59 years and six months. There are also income limits for contribution eligibility. None of these constraints apply to the Canadian plan.

The Role of the C.D. Howe Institute

The leading advocate for the introduction of Tax-Free Savings Accounts in Canada was the C.D. Howe Institute, a non-partisan think-tank based in Toronto that has been an influential voice in public policy since 1958. (C.D. Howe was a senior Liberal Cabinet minister who served in Parliament for 22 years.)

The institute began advocating what it called Tax-Prepaid Savings Plans (TPSPs) as early as February 2001, in a study titled *A New Option for Retirement Savings: Tax-Prepaid Savings Plans*. Authors Jonathan Kesselman, an economics professor at the University of British Columbia, and Finn Poschmann, now director of research at the C.D. Howe Institute, argued that the existing retirement savings system did not work well for lower-income people and increased the likelihood that they would need support from the public purse in their later years. The document attracted little media interest.

In 2003, the institute raised the ante with the publication of a scathing attack on the unfairness of existing savings plans as they relate to low-income Canadians. The paper was titled *New Poverty Traps: Means Testing and Modest-Income Seniors.*[7] The author, Dr. Richard Shillington, holds a doctoral degree in statistics and has been carrying out research into health, social, and economic policies for more than 30 years. His analysis raised serious issues relating to how lower-income seniors who have saved for their retirement are penalized by the way in which government support programs are administered.

Shillington did not mince words. Millions of people who are at or approaching retirement age "are victims of a fraud, however unintentional," he wrote. Saving through RRSPs was likely to make them poorer in retirement, not better off, because most of their RRSP income "will be confiscated by income-tested programs and income taxes."

Government policy-makers were urged to take a close look at the situation and to introduce policies to deal with it as quickly as possible. Specifically, Shillington advocated the creation of TPSPs, similar to the British ISA or the Roth IRA in the United States, which, he said, would meet the retirement savings needs of lower-income Canadians more effectively.

The Liberal government of the day didn't act, so in November 2004, the institute launched yet another initiative. Finn Poschmann and then–senior vice-president and director of research (now CEO) William B.P. Robson co-authored another detailed backgrounder on the topic.

Titled *Saving's Grace: A Framework to Promote Financial Independence for Low-Income Canadians*, the report criticized the federal government for creating a range of savings plans for retirement and education that were better suited to the needs of middle- and upper-income people.[8] Plans such as RRSPs and Registered Pension Plans (RPPs) are not useful for lower-income Canadians, they argued, because the tax savings they offer are negligible (RRSP contributions are treated as deductions, which means the higher a person's bracket, the greater the tax savings). When the money is needed, any withdrawals are taxed, perhaps at a higher rate than the value of the original deduction. Plus, any pension or RRIF payments or RRSP withdrawals reduce eligibility for a range of government benefits, such as the Guaranteed Income Supplement, and government tax credits.

The report urged the federal government to create a new, broadly based, easy-to-understand savings program that would be available to all Canadians, regardless of income. The plan should have as few restrictions as possible, offer generous carry-forward provisions, and allow tax-free withdrawals at any time. Especially important, withdrawals should not be considered as income for means-tested programs, subsidies, and tax credits.

The authors concluded by calling the case for such a plan "compelling." In particular, they said that TPSPs would "let many low-income earners escape the punitive treatment they now suffer at the hands of federal and provincial taxes and benefit claw-backs."

Reading the document today, it seems to me to have been the blueprint used by the Conservatives for the plan introduced in the 2008 budget, right down to the smallest detail. Not surprisingly, Robson and his colleagues were elated. "It was a worthy centrepiece for a budget," he told me. "This is a revolutionary type of savings vehicle for Canada."

Jim Flaherty acknowledged the role the institute played in bringing TFSAs to reality when he visited its headquarters a few days after his budget was unveiled. A framed, autographed copy of his Budget Speech now hangs on the wall in Poschmann's office.

The Next Steps

But the story isn't over yet. There are still some roadblocks to overcome if TFSAs are going to function at maximum efficiency.

Canada has a patchwork quilt of social assistance programs, with conditions and restrictions that vary greatly from one province to another. William Robson described the net effect as "fiendishly complicated and fantastically un-coordinated."

Unless provincial and territorial laws are changed, social programs that apply means tests and/or asset tests to determine eligibility will discourage lower-income people from using TFSAs to save money.

A brief published on September 30, 2008, by the C.D. Howe Institute said that saving money will be "pointless" for anyone who faces clawbacks of social benefits for doing so.[9]

"Having modest savings (as low as $560 in Ontario for a single welfare recipient) can make one ineligible for support programs, like social assistance, which include asset tests," said the brief's authors, John Stapleton and Richard Shillington. "When governments penalize beneficiaries for saving, by reducing program benefits, these programs become traps."

The brief called on the provinces and territories to pass legislation to ensure that TFSAs work properly. This would be achieved by specifying a level up to which people could accumulate TFSA savings without losing benefits, by defining to whom the ceiling will apply (current recipients, new applicants, or both), and by clarifying the conditions under which people can make TFSA withdrawals without jeopardizing social benefits.

The institute also recommended that governments consider building on the TFSA platform by supplementing the savings of lower-income people. The Canada Education Savings Grant, which is added to Registered Education Savings Plan (RESP) contributions, was cited as an example.

So there may be more chapters to come in the TFSA story. But everyone seems to agree that what we now have in place is a valuable first step.

3

The Rules of the Game

Once people understand the concept of TFSAs, they quickly embrace the idea. A Scotiabank survey carried out a few months after the budget announcement found that although awareness was still low at the time, Canadians reacted enthusiastically when the key points of the program were explained.

"Most Canadians single out the tax savings as most appealing, although many also find the flexibility to withdraw funds without compromising contribution room compelling," the survey analysis concluded. "Overall, most Canadians (60%) view the TFSA as an 'ideal savings and investment account' for them."

On the basis of the Scotiabank findings, it appears that TFSAs are going to become immensely popular in the coming months. But you can't play the game if you don't understand the rules. So before we get into the strategies for making TFSAs work most effectively for you, let's review the key points you need to know about these plans and how they differ from RRSPs and RESPs.

Eligibility. You must be a resident of Canada to open a TFSA. You have to provide your Social Insurance Number (SIN) when you open a plan. In order to establish your eligibility, you need to file an income tax return. If you have not filed a return, perhaps because you did not owe any tax, you need to do so or establish your right to have a plan by some other means that is acceptable to the Canada Revenue Agency.

Age limit. Anyone 18 or older can open a TFSA. There is no maximum age. This differs in two important ways from RRSPs. Although most people don't realize it, even a child can open an RRSP as long as he or she has earned income. If your baby girl is chosen to star in a television commercial, the income she earns could be used to open an RRSP. That's not the case with TFSAs—only adults need apply.

At the other end of the age scale, the government does not allow you to hold an RRSP past December 31 of the year in which you turn 71. At that time, you must cash in the plan, convert it to a RRIF, or buy an annuity. That leaves older Canadians without a simple and cheap tax shelter, and as the population ages, more people are becoming concerned about that.

TFSAs are the answer. Since there is no termination date for these plans, you can keep contributing to them (thereby sheltering investment income) until the day you die.

Contribution limit. The initial contribution has been set at $5000 per person in the first year, 2009. The limit is indexed to inflation and, theoretically at least, adjusted annually, but there is some small print in the regulations that makes it unlikely there will be any change in the maximum for the first couple of years and that there will be several years between increases after that.

The Department of Finance decided to move away from the standard annual indexing formula that is used for tax brackets, CPP payments, tax credits, and so forth. Instead, Finance introduced a new type of indexing, which, it says, provides "simplification and certainty." (It will also slow the drain that TFSAs will have on the public purse, but Finance officials say that was not a major factor in the decision.) The TFSA formula requires that indexing be done in increments of $500. This means the limit will be rounded up or down each year. The effect will be to delay the first increase in the TFSA contribution limit until the inflation factor has reached at least $250. Assuming an annual inflation rate of 2 percent, here's what we can expect in changes to the maximum contribution limit over the next few years.

Projected TFSA Contribution Limits

Year	Cumulative inflation factor*	Contribution limit
2010	$5100	$5000
2011	$5202	$5000
2012	$5306	$5500
2013	$5412	$5500
2014	$5520	$5500
2015	$5631	$5500
2016	$5743	$5500
2017	$5858	$6000
2018	$5975	$6000
2019	$6095	$6000
2020	$6217	$6000
2021	$6341	$6500

* Assumes annual inflation rate of 2%.

As you can see, the first increase in the annual maximum contribution will not occur until 2012 unless inflation runs at a higher rate than the Bank of Canada target. It will be 2017 before the limit moves up again, to $6000, and 2021 before we reach $6500.

To put this into perspective, the maximum allowable RRSP contribution for 2009 is $21,000. It will take decades for TFSAs to come anywhere near that. This will become an important consideration when we examine TFSAs versus RRSPs as retirement savings options in Chapter 6.

Contributions in kind. You don't need to have cash to make a TFSA contribution. You can also build a plan through what are known as contributions in kind. This allows you to deposit securities you already own directly to a TFSA. For example, suppose you have money invested in a guaranteed investment certificate (GIC) that does not mature for three years. You can start tax-sheltering the interest immediately by contributing to your plan. You have to pay tax on the interest you earn up to the time you contributed it to your TFSA, but after that all your profit is tax-free. Warning: the GIC face value plus accrued interest cannot exceed your contribution limit.

The rules governing TFSA contributions are the same as those for RRSPs, so there are a couple of points you need to consider before making use of this strategy.

First, if you make a contribution in kind, the Canada Revenue Agency treats the transaction as if you sold the security on the day it went into the plan. This means that if you have a capital gain, for example on a stock or mutual fund, that gain is triggered when you make the contribution and must be declared on your income tax return for that year.

The second point to remember is that, while you have to pay tax on any capital gains created by contributing a security to a TFSA, you may not claim a capital loss. This distortion in the tax rules has burned some people who decided to dump losing stocks into their RRSPs only to discover too late that the loss was not tax-deductible.

So never contribute a money-losing security directly to a TFSA. Sell it first, thereby creating a deductible capital loss, and then put the cash from the sale into the plan.

Swaps. Most of the rules governing TFSAs are the same as those for RRSPs, but the one on swaps is an exception. In the case of RRSPs, you may exchange securities (or cash) from outside a plan for securities of equal value within the plan at any time. However, you are not permitted to do such swaps within TFSAs, at least not instantly.

For example, if you want to exchange shares in a railway company for shares in a bank or vice versa, you would have to withdraw the railway shares (or the cash if you sell them) from your TFSA. You then have to wait until January 1 of the following year, when your contribution limit is adjusted to reflect the withdrawal, to deposit the bank stock.

Overcontributions. These will be taxed at a rate of 1 percent per month, the same penalty that applies to RRSPs. Unlike with RRSPs, however, there is no $2000 lifetime overcontribution allowed.

Deductions. There are none. You do not receive any tax relief for a TFSA contribution. Any money that goes into a plan is on an after-tax basis (RESPs operate the same way). This is a major difference between TFSAs and RRSPs—one that will certainly cause a lot of head-scratching as people decide which plan they should contribute to.

Carry-forwards. The rules are similar to those for RRSPs in that any unused contribution room may be carried forward indefinitely. For example, if you contribute only $2000 to a new TFSA in 2009, your limit in 2010 will be $8000 ($5000 plus the $3000 carried forward from 2009).

TFSA year-end. For purposes of contributions and carry-forwards, TFSAs operate on a calendar-year basis, so the annual cut-off date is December 31. This means TFSAs use the same clock as RESPs. (RRSP contributions, by contrast, may be made up to 60 days after the end of the calendar year.)

Number of plans. As with RRSPs, there is no limit on the number of TFSAs you can open. But common sense suggests that you limit yourself to one plan for ease of administration. If you decide to open a second TFSA, make sure you have a good reason for doing so.

Withdrawals. You can take money out of a TFSA at any time, with no tax consequences. You don't even have to declare it on your income tax return—it is like withdrawing money from your bank savings account. And here is an interesting twist: Unlike with RRSPs, any amount you withdraw is added back to your contribution limit for the next year.

Let's suppose you accumulate $20,000 in a TFSA between now and 2013. At that point, you decide to draw out $15,000 to help pay for a new car. Assuming that the annual contribution limit at that time is $5500, your personal limit for 2014 will be $20,500—the basic maximum plus the amount you took out of the plan for the car purchase.

Taxes. Although you don't get a tax deduction when you contribute, all withdrawals from your TFSA are tax-free. The investment income earned within the plan is fully sheltered forever—unlike RRSPs, where all investment income earned within a plan is taxed at your marginal taxation rate when you withdraw it. TFSAs thus provide a way to earn investment income without incurring any tax liability, now or in the future.

Reporting. Although TFSAs aren't taxable, the Canada Revenue Agency will need to keep tabs on your plan in order to determine how much you are allowed to contribute in any given year. The government has placed the reporting responsibility in the hands of the financial institution that administers your plan by requiring it to file an annual information return. This includes all contributions, withdrawals, and transfers made during the year as well as the value of the plan's assets at the beginning and end of the year. Assuming the system works, you won't be saddled with any additional paperwork. Your annual notice of assessment will contain a section advising you of the status of your TFSA—in the same way as your RRSP contribution room is currently shown.

Income testing. TFSA withdrawals are not considered as income. So they don't compromise your eligibility for income-tested tax credits such as the Age Credit, the Canada Child Tax Benefit, or the GST tax credit. You can withdraw money from TFSAs without affecting Employment Insurance benefits. For older Canadians, TFSA withdrawals don't affect their eligibility for programs such as the Guaranteed Income Supplement (GIS) and don't result in Old Age Security (OAS) clawbacks.

This is very important for lower-income seniors. Under current rules, GIS payments are cut by 50 cents for every $1 worth of income a recipient receives, including the income from RRSP withdrawals and RRIF payments. So low-income seniors receiving GIS see their payments eroded because they made the effort to save a little for retirement. That's why, in his 2003 paper, Dr. Richard Shillington of the C.D. Howe Institute suggested that people who expect to qualify for GIS should not make RRSP contributions and advised the government to introduce a TFSA-like program instead. It took six years, but here it is.

Investments. TFSAs are highly flexible when it comes to the investments you can choose. The rules for qualified securities are the same as those applied to RRSPs. Almost anything is allowed: guaranteed investment certificates, mutual funds, stocks (Canadian and foreign), bonds, gold, and cash. Even shares in a small business are eligible under certain conditions. The major exceptions (as with RRSPs) are real estate and non-arm's-length investments. If you are uncertain whether an investment qualifies, get professional advice before going ahead, because the penalties for including non-eligible investments in a TFSA can be severe.

Deposit insurance. Certain types of TFSA deposits are covered up to $100,000 by the Canada Deposit Insurance Corporation (CDIC), including cash, term deposits, and guaranteed investment certificates. But as a general rule, most securities, including stocks and mutual funds, are not covered. That includes money market funds. For complete details on federal deposit insurance, visit www.cdic.ca.

Interest deductibility. You may borrow money to invest in a TFSA, but you cannot claim the interest on the loan as a tax deduction. These rules are the same as for RRSPs.

Spousal plans. You can set up a TFSA for your spouse or common-law partner and contribute to it. Unlike RRSPs, a contribution to a spousal TFSA will not count against your own contribution limit. However, your spouse or partner must have room available.

Income splitting. The usual income attribution rules do not apply to TFSAs. This means one spouse can provide the money for the other to open an account without penalty. So even if the other spouse has no income or savings, he or she can have a TFSA. Over the years, this could lead to big tax savings for families. See Chapter 9 for more information.

Marriage breakdown. TFSA assets can be transferred from the plan of one spouse or partner to the plan of the other in the event of a marriage breakdown. However, in this case, the person from whom the money is transferred is not given new contribution room to compensate. Any such transfer does not count against the contribution room of the spouse or partner who receives the money.

Transfers. You can transfer assets from one of your own TFSAs to another one. This is called a "qualifying transfer." If you want to move the money into an RRSP, you can make a tax-free withdrawal from the TFSA and contribute directly to the RRSP, which will generate a tax deduction.

Loan collateral. Unlike RRSPs, the new plans can be used as collateral for loans. This could be useful in a situation where you suddenly need cash to deal with an emergency, but the money in your TFSA is not accessible, perhaps because it has been invested in a locked-in GIC. If the lender is satisfied that the assets in the plan are sound, the TFSA can serve as collateral for a cash advance.

There is one important exception. In order to prevent TFSA contribution room from being "sold" or "rented," any loan agreement must be on an arm's-length basis. If the propriety of a loan is questioned, you have to be able to show that the loan was not intended to "enable another person or partnership to benefit from the exemption from tax" provided by the TFSA exemption.

Living abroad. If you leave Canada after opening a TFSA, you can maintain the account and continue to make withdrawals. However, you have to check whether such withdrawals would be regarded as tax-free by the country in which you are residing. You may not make any new contributions while you are out of the country and no new contribution room will accrue.

Death. When you die, the assets in your TFSA can be transferred to the plan of your spouse or common-law partner. Things get a little more complicated when the last spouse or partner dies, but essentially all of the assets in a TFSA at the time of death can pass to the next generation tax-free. More details are presented in Chapter 10.

4

The "Magic" of TFSAs

Quick now, what is often referred to as the "eighth wonder of the world"?

The answer is compound interest. It's a simple but powerful way to get rich, provided you have time and a little self-discipline.

Before we go any further, let me clarify an important point. Although the term generally used is *compound interest,* what we are really talking about is compounded profits from investment income of any kind. That can include dividends, rental income, capital gains, and anything else you earn from your invested money. So for the purposes of this discussion, I'll use the all-encompassing term of *compound income.*

Compound income simply amounts to profit earning more profit. If you invest $1 at 4 percent, after one year you'll have $1.04. Now you'll start to earn income on that extra four cents as well as on your original dollar. It doesn't happen quickly, but over the years, that can add up to a lot of money.

The Rule of 72 is a classic way to calculate how long it will take for an amount of money to double in value through compounding. To use it, simply divide the return on the invested money by 72. For instance, if you invest $1000 at an annual rate of return of

4 percent, it will take 18 years for your money to double (72 ÷ 4). But if your money earns 6 percent, it will double in only 12 years (72 ÷ 6).

Of course, this assumes that you get to keep all the investment income for yourself. In reality, the government keeps dipping its sticky fingers into your profits. And that's been the big problem for Canadians until now. We've had no way to fully benefit from the magic of compound income in this country because Ottawa and the provinces are always taking a share of the pie.

You may ask: What about RRSPs? While it's true that any investment income that is earned in retirement savings plans is tax-sheltered, you're hit with a big tax bite when you take the money out.

For example, suppose you contribute $1000 a year to an RRSP over 30 years and invest the money in guaranteed investment certificates that pay an average annual return of 5 percent. At the end of that time, the plan is valued at $69,761. Subtracting your $30,000 in contributions, you have earned investment income totalling almost $40,000.

But as soon as you start taking money out of that RRSP, the government swoops in and taxes it. If you are in the 30 percent bracket, you'll give back $12,000 of the income you've earned over all those years to the tax folks. You get to keep only $28,000 for yourself. The 5 percent you thought you earned ended up only being about 4 percent in after-tax terms. If you are in a 40 percent bracket, your after-tax profit drops to $24,000. Suddenly, compounding doesn't seem quite so magical anymore.

Tax-Free Savings Accounts change everything. For the first time, we have access to an investment vehicle that allows us to obtain the full benefit of compounding. The income we earn in a TFSA is 100 percent ours to keep. No part of it is taxed away.

Here's a table that illustrates what this means in terms of wealth building over time and shows the value of the TFSA at the end of various time frames. I've assumed an average annual compound rate of return of 5 percent in all cases.

TFSA Growth at 5 Percent

Annual contribution	10 years	20 years	30 years	40 years
$1000	$13,207	$34,719	$69,761	$126,840
$2000	$26,414	$69,439	$139,522	$253,680
$3000	$39,620	$104,158	$209,282	$380,519
$4000	$52,827	$138,877	$279,043	$507,359
$5000	$66,034	$173,596	$348,804	$634,199

Assumption: Contribution is made at start of year.

In case you're wondering, it would take 50 years for the value of the plan to surpass $1 million based on an annual contribution of $5000. But with life expectancy increasing, readers who are 25 today have a realistic hope of achieving that $1 million. Also, remember that couples can save twice as much. We'll examine the implications of that in Chapter 12.

Take a close look at the numbers in this table. There are two key points to take away.

Start young. Compounding is like a rolling snowball. It takes time to gather speed and mass. The more years a plan has to grow, the more impressive the returns will be.

Look at the $1000 line in the table. After one decade, the plan has only added $3207 to your original $10,000 in contributions. But after 20 years, the investment income earned within the plan has ballooned to $14,719 ($34,719 minus $20,000 in contributions). After 40 years, the magic of compounding has given you a total, tax-free profit of $86,840!

So the sooner you begin, the more effectively a TFSA can work for you. Obviously, none of us can turn back time. But however old you are today, the same basic rule applies: The sooner you begin, the more effective a TFSA is.

Contribute as much as you can. Slide your eyes down each column. You'll see that the more money you contribute annually, the more profitable a TFSA becomes over the years. If you double the annual contribution from $1000 to $2000, your profit from compounding also doubles after the first decade, from $3207 to $6414. If you are able to contribute the initial maximum amount of $5000 annually, your 10-year profit increases to $16,034. (Of course, these figures assume no withdrawals are made along the way.)

The powerhouse effect of combining high contributions with many years of growth is apparent in the cell on the bottom right of the table. This shows you how much money is in a plan after 40 years of growth at 5 percent with an annual contribution of $5000. The total is $634,199, which means your tax-free profit after deducting all contributions is $434,199. That's a nice nest-egg to draw on in retirement!

An Extra Point of Return

Now let's play with these numbers a little. The next table shows you the value of a TFSA if you are able to add one percentage point of annual return over the years, moving from 5 percent to 6 percent.

TFSA Growth at 6 Percent

Annual contribution	10 years	20 years	30 years	40 years
$1000	$13,972	$38,993	$83,802	$164,048
$2000	$27,943	$77,985	$167,603	$328,095
$3000	$41,915	$116,978	$251,405	$492,143
$4000	$55,887	$155,971	$335,207	$656,191
$5000	$69,858	$194,964	$419,008	$820,238

Assumption: Contribution is made at start of year.

What a difference a percentage point makes over time! After a decade, that extra return doesn't translate into a large profit gain—at the $1000 annual contribution level, the additional growth is only $765, which suggests that for older people the added risk involved may not be worth it. But look what happens as the years pass and the magic of compounding takes hold. Staying with the $1000 contributor, at the end of the second decade the additional gain is $4274. After 40 years, this person is ahead by $37,208 because he or she invested the money wisely and earned one percentage point more.

Here again, the more you contribute, the greater the impact of the extra percentage point of return. An annual contribution of $5000 that is invested to earn an average annual gain of 5 percent grows to $634,199 after 40 years. But at 6 percent, the TFSA is worth $820,238 at that stage. The extra percentage point has given you an additional $186,039 to help fund your retirement. Now that's impressive!

End of Year Contributions

Finally, let's look at one more set of numbers. The tables we've looked at so far assume that TFSA contributions are made at the start of each calendar year, on January 1. Most people, however, tend to put things off. So let's see what happens if the contributions are delayed to the last minute, to December 31 of the same year. Here's what our 6 percent table would look like in those circumstances.

TFSA Growth at 6 Percent

Annual contribution	10 years	20 years	30 years	40 years
$1000	$13,181	$36,786	$79,058	$154,762
$2000	$26,362	$73,571	$158,116	$309,524
$3000	$39,542	$110,357	$237,175	$464,286
$4000	$52,723	$147,142	$316,233	$619,048
$5000	$65,904	$183,928	$395,291	$773,804

Assumption: Contribution is made at end of year.

This may be difficult to believe, but waiting until the end of each year to make a TFSA contribution can end up costing you tens of thousands of dollars in lost profit (the same applies to RRSPs, by the way). Again, you don't notice much of an impact in the early years, but as the compounding snowball begins to gain momentum, the price of delaying starts to add up.

The person who contributes $3000 annually on December 31 of each year has $6621 less profit after 20 years than someone who makes the same contribution 12 months earlier, on January 1.

As we move out to 40 years, the impact of delaying a contribution really hits hard. Someone who puts $5000 a year into a TFSA on January 1 of each year over that time will have a plan worth $820,238. The person who waits until year-end will have only $773,804. That's a difference of more than $46,000, proving once again that procrastination can be expensive.

Action Summary

1. Start immediately. Set up a TFSA as soon as you can. The more years your money can grow tax-sheltered, the wealthier you will be.
2. Contribute as much as possible. Any amount is better than nothing, but if you stretch a little, the reward at the end will be much greater.
3. Contribute early. Don't wait until New Year's Eve to make your annual contribution. Get the money into the plan as early in the year as possible.
4. Within reason, aim for a higher return. Don't take needless risks with your TFSA money, but don't be overly conservative either, especially if you are under 50. An extra percentage point of profit will add thousands of dollars to your wealth over the years.

5

Saving for a Rainy Day

Every financial expert will tell you the same thing: All families should have an emergency cash reserve to help them get through difficult times. The problem is that in recent years few people have been paying attention to this basic rule of money management. The idea of putting something aside for a rainy day doesn't resonate when the sun is shining all the time.

In the United States, the savings rate has fallen to close to zero and is threatening to slip into negative territory, a phenomenon unheard of since the Great Depression of the 1930s. Canadians have also succumbed to the same virus, with Statistics Canada reporting that at the end of June 2008, the average household was carrying a debt load of $1.25 for every $1.00 of personal disposable income.[1]

The sub-prime mortgage disaster in the United States was a chilling lesson in just how destructive too much debt can be. Americans lost their homes to foreclosures at a higher rate than at any time since the 1930s. Thousands of decent people ended up on the street because they could not meet their mortgage payments. Had they put some money into an emergency savings account over the years, they might have been able to survive.

I believe that we are going to see more emphasis on saving in the next few years as people realize the danger of overextending themselves. As it happens, the fortuitous timing of the introduction of Tax-Free Savings Accounts makes saving easier and more financially attractive.

Until now, there has not been any truly effective way to build an emergency fund. Putting the money in a regular bank savings account is easy and safe, but it pays no return to speak of. In fact, when inflation is taken into account, your emergency fund probably loses some value each year.

A high-interest savings account is a better choice, but unless it is inside a TFSA, the return on your savings will still be negligible after taxes and inflation are deducted. For example, suppose you put $1000 of emergency money into a high-interest savings account that pays 3 percent a year. You are in the 30 percent tax bracket, and the inflation rate is 2 percent. Your statement shows that you earn $30 a year on your money. But the government grabs $9 of that in taxes, and inflation reduces the buying power of your savings by $20, to $980. Your real return on your savings for that year is only $1! That works out to 0.1 percent. "Why bother?" you may ask.

Some people have tried to get around this dilemma by using their RRSPs as an emergency fund; it's an approach I suggested in my book *Get Control of Your Money*, which was published in 2003. The RRSP strategy offers the advantage of an immediate tax refund and postpones the tax bite on investment income until the money is withdrawn. But the downside is that this approach could actually end up costing you more in the end. That's because you may have to withdraw cash for an emergency at a time when you are in a higher tax bracket than you were when you originally contributed the money. Also, a withholding tax of anywhere from 10 percent to 30 percent applies to all RRSP withdrawals except in Quebec, where the minimum is 21 percent and the maximum 35 percent. Although you'll get credit for any tax withheld when you file your annual tax return, it means you won't have access to all your money at a time when you may need it most.

The ideal emergency fund allows you quick access to your cash whenever you need it while providing tax-sheltering for the income your money earns in the meantime. That's the precise description of a TFSA. These plans are the perfect vehicles for building your emergency savings account, which means that every family should have one.

If you already have an emergency fund, your first step should be to open a TFSA (and one for your spouse or partner as well) and move the money into the plan. If you have not created such a fund, now is the ideal time to start. It should be the first priority in building your TFSA.

Gillian Riley, Scotiabank's managing director and head of retail deposits, puts it this way: "When thinking about the TFSA and how Canadians can apply it to their personal financial situation, I would recommend that they look at how they use their traditional savings account and consider using the TFSA instead to earn tax-free growth. The TFSA is a tool that should inspire Canadians to save because of its added benefits and versatility."

Of course, the best time to build an emergency fund is when your budget is under control and you can free up some cash. The problem is that people always find something on which to spend any extra money they earn. When budgets are stretched, saving becomes even harder. Sure, an emergency fund may be a fine idea. But after paying the household bills, the mortgage, the car loan, the dentist, and all the other bills, there's nothing left over.

So you must make building your emergency fund a priority. You have to decide that this is a financial cushion your family simply must have and that one way or another you're going to make it happen, even if it means some sacrifices. That's why it needs to be included as an integral part of the family budget. Commitment is half the battle.

How Big a Fund?

Generally, I recommend your emergency fund be equal to at least three months' worth of family take-home pay (after tax). Some experts counsel having a six-month reserve, and I have recently seen some popular U.S. financial gurus suggesting that eight months' worth of income be set aside.

To put this in dollar terms, let's look at the case of a childless couple, with each person earning an income of $60,000. So the total family income before taxes is $120,000 a year. The after-tax amount will vary depending on the value of the tax credits the couple has available to them and where they live due to different provincial rates across the country. An Ontario couple with only basic personal tax credits will have an after-tax combined income of about $94,000, based on 2008 tax rates. If we use the three-month formula, they should have at least $23,500 in their emergency fund.

In contrast, a single person living in Nova Scotia who has a taxable income of only $35,000 a year and an after-tax income of $28,300 would need a minimum emergency reserve of about $7000.

These examples illustrate that there is no "right" amount for everyone. Much depends on your personal situation. Income is not the only factor to consider; you must also take into account your financial risk level. A single-income family whose breadwinner is an autoworker in Ontario should try to put more money aside than a couple in Alberta who both work in the public sector because the risk of job loss is much higher in the automotive sector and there isn't a second income to fall back on. A family whose main wage earner has a history of illness should have a larger emergency fund than one in which the primary breadwinner is healthy. Families with children need to have more money in reserve than those who are childless.

Putting some cash aside each month for an emergency fund may seem daunting when you're planning a budget. But if you actually have to draw on the fund at some point, you will be thankful you made the effort. So where do you find the money?

I said earlier that commitment is half the battle when it comes to creating an emergency fund. The other half is execution. One way to achieve this goal is to set up a pre-authorized savings plan at your financial institution. Tell them to put aside 3 percent to 5 percent of your income each month (whatever you decide is appropriate) and deposit it into your TFSA. Even if the amount is small, I urge you to start the process. Then add to your savings every time a family member gets a salary increase or you receive some windfall money, such as a tax refund.

Since everyone is allowed to set up a TFSA, a couple can put as much as $10,000 into their plans in the first year. That is a good start toward an emergency fund; for a family with a low financial risk, it might even be enough.

Investment Options

Once you've started saving for an emergency fund, the question is where to invest the cash. There are two priorities to take into account. The first is safety: This is your "rainy day" money, so you don't want to put it at risk. The stock market meltdown that we experienced in the fall of 2008 was a painful reminder of the dangers of aggressive investing.

Your second priority is accessibility. Unless the money is available to you immediately, you don't have a true emergency fund.

This means you should not invest in any type of locked-in security, such as a non-redeemable guaranteed investment certificate. While such GICs are safe (they are covered by deposit insurance up to the legal limit) and offer more attractive interest rates than savings accounts, they will tie up your money for anywhere up to 10 years, depending on the maturity date (one-year to five-year terms are the most common). That makes them non-starters for emergency funds.

Redeemable GICs are a better choice in that you can get your money out before maturity if needed. However, you'll pay an interest rate penalty if you do, which may inhibit you from using the money even when it is badly needed.

Some financial institutions offer one-year cashable GICs that can be redeemed at any time without penalty. This makes them the most suitable type of GIC for an emergency fund, but there is one big drawback—the interest rate offered may be even less than that paid by a high-interest savings account.

A high-interest account is certainly a decent option for your emergency fund. The rates paid by these accounts are much better than those offered by conventional savings accounts. You won't get rich by saving with them, but your money will be safe, you'll be able to withdraw it at any time, and the interest you earn will be tax-free. These accounts are especially good choices when interest rates are moving higher, since their rates are adjusted frequently.

If you decide this is the route you want to go, be sure to open your TFSA at a financial institution that offers a high-interest account that does not have a prohibitive minimum requirement.

Check the rates being offered by various companies. For example, at the time of writing, one financial institution was paying 2.75 percent on its high-interest savings account while another was offering a quarter-point more, at 3 percent. Many people will forgo an extra quarter-point of interest for the convenience of dealing with their current bank. But do some comparison shopping and make sure your account is covered by deposit insurance.

Money Market Funds

If you want to aim for a slightly higher return, a money market fund (MMF) could be the answer. MMFs invest in short-term securities with an average term to maturity of less than 90 days (although they may hold notes with maturities out to one year). To qualify as a Canadian money market fund, at least 95 percent of the assets must be invested in Canadian-dollar securities.

MMFs have long been considered to be almost risk-free. However, nothing should be taken for granted these days. Even theoretically safe short-term notes can lose some or all of their value, and MMFs are not protected by deposit insurance. In 2007, National Bank had to put up $2 billion to bail out its MMFs as well as some Altamira funds after they were caught holding tainted asset-backed commercial paper (ABCP) in the wake of the U.S. sub-prime mortgage crash.

The Canadian Securities Administrators (CSA), which brings together all the provincial regulators, announced in September 2008 that it was looking into the extent to which Canadian MMFs might be exposed to high-risk U.S. debt securities, such as short-term notes issued by failed Lehman Brothers and Washington Mutual. The "fact-finding review," as it was called, was conducted in association with the Investment Industry Regulatory

Organization of Canada (IIROC), which has oversight responsibility for brokerage houses.

The announcement came after the U.S. government had to step in and guarantee MMFs in that country for losses up to $50 billion after the giant Reserve Primary Fund "broke the buck," that is, it reduced its net asset value to less than $1 because of losses due to its position in Lehman Brothers notes. (Canadian MMFs normally have a net asset value of $10.) At the time of writing, no Canadian MMF appeared to be in difficulty and none had dropped below par.

But don't automatically assume your money market fund is safe. Ask your financial adviser (or the fund company itself if you don't have an adviser) what type of assets are held by the MMF you are considering. If you are not satisfied with the answer, switch to another MMF or to a high-interest savings account, which will be covered by deposit insurance.

The safest MMFs are those that invest only in federal or provincial treasury bills or government-guaranteed securities. The Altamira T-Bill Fund is an example. Most of the major banks also offer T-bill funds.

Safety is obviously a priority when it comes to choosing an MMF, but there are other considerations. Money market funds are not created equal. They may look alike, in the sense that they all have a fixed price of $10 and they all invest in short-term securities. But that's where the similarities end. In fact, there are some very good money market funds, some very bad ones, and a whole lot of mediocre ones. Obviously, you want a good one, so here's what to look for.

No sales commission. Never pay a sales commission to buy or sell money market fund units. There are plenty of good no-load funds around. I received an email recently from a distraught investor whose adviser had put his money into two MMFs on a deferred sales charge (DSC) basis. That meant that if he wanted to withdraw cash within the first six years of holding, he would be dinged with a redemption charge. He blamed himself for not paying closer attention, but I blamed his financial adviser, who had obviously acted in his own interest (he got a commission this way) and not in the interest of his client. Don't allow yourself to fall into that trap. MMFs should be commission-free, in and out.

Low fees. Returns on money market funds are historically quite low, so it's important to select a fund that will give you the most bang for your buck. This means avoiding funds with high management expense ratios (MERs). These ratios represent the cost to the fund of management fees and expenses and they come right off your return. For example, if a money fund generates a gross profit of 4 percent in a given year and has an MER of 0.5 percent, your return is 3.5 percent. But if the MER is 1.5 percent (and some are even higher), your return is only 2.5 percent. Don't have your pocket picked in this way!

Whatever way you decide to build your emergency fund within a TFSA, always remember the two most important principles: make sure that your money is safe and that you can get at it quickly if needed.

Action Summary

1. Every family should have an emergency fund. A TFSA offers an ideal way to build one.
2. Choose an investment that offers both safety and quick access to your money if it is needed.

3. Avoid GICs or any other security that locks you in for a long time.
4. If you invest in a money market fund, select one that has low ongoing fees and no sales commissions.

6

TFSAs or RRSPs?

The first question many people ask about TFSAs is whether they should use TFSAs or RRSPs for retirement saving.

There's no easy answer. TFSAs provide a valuable new option for retirement planning, but how they are best used will depend on each person's circumstances.

To begin with, it's important to understand that TFSAs and RRSPs are two different creatures from a tax and savings perspective. In the jargon of economists, TFSAs are so-called TEE plans—taxed, exempt, exempt. That means the money going into the plan has already been taxed, but earnings within a TFSA are tax-exempt, as are all withdrawals.

In contrast, RRSPs are so-called EET plans—exempt, exempt, taxed. Contributions are tax-free because they generate an offsetting deduction. Investment income earned within an RRSP is also tax-free. But all the money that comes out is taxed at your marginal rate, regardless of its source. That means you'll pay more tax on capital gains and dividends earned within an RRSP than you would if those same profits were generated in a non-registered account.

In the Budget Papers that explained the TFSA concept in detail, the Department of Finance included an example that suggested there is no after-tax advantage in using either TFSAs or RRSPs for retirement savings. Based on their assumptions, both produced the same net after-tax return and both were equally superior to saving in a non-registered account. Here is the illustration they used.[1]

Net Proceeds from Saving in a TFSA Relative to Other Savings Vehicles

	TFSA	RRSP	Unregistered savings
Pre-tax income	$1000	$1000	$1000
Tax (40% rate)	$400	-	$400
Net contribution[1]	$600	$1000	$600
Investment income (20 years at 5.5%)	$1151	$1918	$707[2]
Gross proceeds (net contribution + investment income)	$1751	$2918	$1307
Tax (40% rate)	-	$1167	-
Net proceeds	$1751	$1751	$1307
Net annual after-tax rate of return[3] (%)	5.5	5.5	4.0

[1]Forgone consumption (saving) is $600 in all cases. In the RRSP case, the person contributes $1000 but receives a $400 reduction in tax, thereby sacrificing net consumption of $600.
[2]For unregistered saving case, tax rate on investment income is 28%, representing a weighted average tax rate on an investment portfolio comprised of 30% dividends, 30% capital gains, and 40% interest.
[3]Measured in relation to forgone consumption of $600. Assumes annual nominal pre-tax rate of return is 5.5% invested for 20 years.

This example assumes a contribution of $1000 to each of three different accounts—a TFSA, an RRSP, and an unregistered investment plan. But it is important to read the first footnote to the table to understand the rationale the Department of Finance used for the after-tax rate of return calculation. The figure is not based on the amount invested but rather on what Finance defines as "forgone consumption." This is the amount actually saved.

In all cases, the investor starts with a gross of $1000. With the TFSA and the unregistered account, $400 is taken by taxes, leaving $600 in savings. That's straightforward enough, but the RRSP calculation is more complex: It appears at first glance that $1000 is the amount saved because that's what is paid into the plan and no tax is assessed because of the deduction generated. But the accepted way to make apples-to-apples comparisons in such situations is to examine it from the perspective of how much money a person could have spent if he or she had not made an investment. Using this approach, the "forgone consumption" is $600 in all cases. So the calculation of returns in all three scenarios is based on $600, although that number does not show up on the Net Contribution line in the RRSP column. For consistency, I'll stay with that approach in the analysis that follows.

Referring to the Finance table, you'll see it shows that the average annual compound rate of return for both a TFSA and an RRSP is 5.5 percent and the tax rate going in and coming out is 40 percent.

But if you change those basic assumptions, the end result can be quite different. Let's manipulate the numbers and consider the various outcomes. We'll begin by assuming that the contributor's marginal tax rate is lower in retirement than when she was working. We'll consider only a TFSA versus an RRSP because the results in an unregistered account don't change. Here is what happens, again using the "forgone consumption" of $600 as the base.

Net Proceeds from Saving in a TFSA Relative to an RRSP When the Final Tax Rate Is Lower

	TFSA	RRSP
Pre-tax income	$1000	$1000
Tax (40% rate)	$400	-
Net contribution	$600	$1000
Investment income (20 years at 5.5%)	$1151	$1918
Gross proceeds (net contribution + investment income)	$1751	$2918
Tax (30% rate)	-	$875
Net proceeds	$1751	$2043
Net annual after-tax rate of return (%)	5.5	6.3

In this case, as the table shows, the RRSP is clearly the better choice. It produces an average annual compound rate of return of 6.3 percent over 20 years compared to 5.5 percent for a TFSA. This means that higher-income people who expect their tax rate to be lower after retirement should top up their RRSPs first before investing in a TFSA.

Now let's see what happens when the tax rate after retirement is higher than when a person was working.

Net Proceeds from Saving in a TFSA Relative to an RRSP When the Final Tax Rate Is Higher

	TFSA	RRSP
Pre-tax income	$1000	$1000
Tax (30% rate)	$300	–
Net contribution	$700	$1000

	TFSA	RRSP
Investment income (20 years at 5.5%)	$1342	$1918
Gross proceeds (net contribution + investment income)	$2042	$2918
Tax (40% rate)	–	$1167
Net proceeds	$2042	$1751
Net annual after-tax rate of return (%)	5.5	4.7

Because the tax rate is lower, the "forgone consumption" in this case is $700, so that becomes the basis for the rate of return calculation. As the table shows, a TFSA is the better choice in this case, with an average annual compound rate of return of 5.5 percent, versus 4.7 percent for an RRSP.

So to sum up:

If you expect your tax rate after retirement to be the same as it is now, TFSAs and RRSPs will produce the same net result.

If you expect your tax rate after retirement to be less than it is now, top up your RRSP before opening a TFSA.

If you expect your tax rate after retirement to be higher than it is now, saving in a TFSA will produce a better return than making an RRSP contribution.

When TFSAs Are Clearly Better

There are certain situations in which TFSAs are clearly a better choice than RRSPs for retirement planning purposes. Here are three of them.

Pension plan members. Anyone who belongs to a pension plan loses RRSP contribution room because of the "pension adjustment" (PA). This is a complex calculation that takes into account the amount contributed to a pension plan by you and your employer, as well as the retirement benefit you will eventually receive. The more generous the plan, the higher the PA will be.

Anyone with a defined benefit pension plan (one that provides guaranteed retirement income based on a combination of salary and years of service) is likely to have a high PA. People in higher income brackets may find they have little or no RRSP room left after the PA has been deducted.

In this situation, TFSAs offer a valuable new alternative for supplementing pension income. By making the maximum possible contribution each year, you can build a tax-paid nest egg that will provide extra income that can be used for travel, a home in the Sunbelt, helping your kids buy a first home, a grandchild's post-secondary education, or anything else you may want to do after you stop work.

There's another reason to set up a TFSA to add to your retirement savings: It's a form of pension insurance. In the past, North Americans took their pension plans for granted. Not any more. In recent years, many pension plans have been forced to cut benefits because the funding was no longer there to support them.

Financially troubled US Airways was forced to cut pension benefits for its pilots by as much as 70 percent. Other major American airlines have sought to do the same, as did Air Canada while it was under creditor protection (it didn't succeed). Bethlehem Steel went into bankruptcy, leaving behind US$3.6 billion in unpaid obligations to its plan.

The Pension Benefit Guaranty Corporation (PBGC), which provides limited support to U.S. pensioners who have had their payments cut or suspended, reported in 2008 that there was a

US$14 billion gap between its assets and the liabilities it was facing. In testimony before a House of Representatives subcommittee in September 2008, PBGC director Charles E.F. Millard said that at the end of 2007, the agency was paying benefits to 630,000 retirees and beneficiaries in terminated underfunded plans. "Another 534,000 participants in these plans will become eligible to start receiving benefits in the future," he added.

The PBGC website[2] is replete with reports of failed pension plans being bailed out or taken over. A few recent examples:

> September 30, 2008: The PBGC assumes responsibility for the pensions of nearly 1200 workers and retirees of Marcal Paper Mills Inc. of Elmwood Park, New Jersey.
>
> September 19, 2008: The PBGC takes over a pension plan that covers more than 950 former employees of Consumers Distributing Inc. in New York.
>
> September 18, 2008: The agency announces it has assumed responsibility for the pension plan that covers about 760 former employees of publisher Rand McNally & Co., of Skokie, Illinois.
>
> July 29, 2008: The PBGC says it will cover the pensions of more than 1500 workers and retirees of Auburn Memorial Hospital, a non-profit medical centre in Auburn, New York.
>
> June 24, 2008: The PBGC announces it will assume responsibility for the pensions of about 700 workers and retirees of Rockford Products Corp. in Rockford, Illinois.

The list goes on and on, but you get the idea. Pension plans in the United States are failing at an alarming rate, putting increasing pressure on an already cash-strapped government agency.

Don't be deluded into thinking this is just an American problem. It can happen here, and even the biggest Canadian plans are not immune. But in Canada, we have no equivalent to the PBGC. That means there is no government agency to protect you if your own pension plan runs into financial trouble. (Ontario has a provincial program, but the benefits it covers are minimal.)

In September 2008, the Ontario Teachers' Pension Plan, which has more than $100 billion in assets, asked its members to give up part of their inflation-protection indexing to help deal with a $12.7 billion funding deficit.[3] If it can happen to teachers, who's safe?

The message is: Take nothing for granted. TFSAs provide an opportunity to backstop your pension plan with what amounts to your own pension insurance policy. Take advantage of it.

Modest-income Canadians. As we saw in Chapter 2, the primary rationale for the C.D. Howe Institute's strong advocacy of TFSAs was to provide an alternative retirement savings program that would better meet the needs of low-income people.

In all its reports on the subject, the institute was critical of the way in which low-income savers were penalized by government policies when the time came to draw on their RRSP or RRIF accounts. The most scathing denouncement was contained in Dr. Richard Shillington's 2003 paper, *New Poverty Traps: Means Testing and Modest-Income Seniors.*

"The primary beneficiary of this saving will be the federal and provincial governments because most of the income from it will be confiscated by income-tested programs and income taxes,"

Shillington wrote. "To the extent that these households have been misled, they have been defrauded."[4]

The report makes a clear distinction between the value of RRSP saving for higher-income Canadians, who will ultimately benefit from their plans, and lower-income people, who will not. Shillington's message was that all those with less than $100,000 in retirement assets are "futile savers" because they will probably need financial support from governments after they stop work. Those benefits will be reduced or even eliminated if there is any income from RRSPs and RRIFs. (Remember: Every dollar in income from one of those plans reduces a Guaranteed Income Supplement benefit by 50 cents.)

Using a TFSA instead of an RRSP eliminates that problem, at least on the federal level. The federal government has ensured that TFSA withdrawals are not treated as income, nor are they taken into account when calculating eligibility for GIS, tax credits, Employment Insurance, and so forth. (At the time of writing, the provinces still have to take action to provide similar treatment for programs they deliver.)

Clearly, anyone with a modest income should favour TFSAs over RRSPs for retirement savings purposes, even when the amounts being put aside are small.

No earned income. You cannot make an RRSP contribution unless you have what the government calls "earned income." Mostly, this is money earned from employment, but some other types of income, such as rents and alimony, also qualify. Investment income does not qualify as earned income, nor do pension payments, whether they are from the government or from a private plan.

If you don't have any earned income, or if the amount is small, TFSAs become your retirement savings vehicle by default. That's because you don't need any earned income at all to make a TFSA contribution.

Many years ago, the typical Canadian family had one wage earner, usually the husband. The wife remained at home and raised the couple's children. Such families are less common today, but they still exist. In this situation, the wife is not able to save independently for her retirement through an RRSP because she has no earned income. The husband can make a spousal contribution on her behalf, of course, but unless he is willing to do so, she is out of luck. If the marriage breaks down or the husband mishandles the savings, the wife could be in financial difficulty in her later years.

Now she has an option: a TFSA. She does not need to have earned income to set up a personal retirement account. If she has some money of her own (perhaps from an inheritance from her parents), she can contribute some of it to the plan. Alternatively, her husband can give her the money to contribute, since income attribution rules will not apply in this case.

When RRSPs Are Better

There are some situations in which an RRSP is a better option than a TFSA—in fact, it may be the only choice. One example is a child or teenager with earned income. You must be 18 or older to open a TFSA, but there is no age limit for RRSPs. As long as a person has earned income, that person can have an RRSP account.

Most people don't realize this, so they pass up opportunities to encourage their children to put some of their earnings, however minimal they may be, into an RRSP. I have a 16-year-old granddaughter who had a summer job at Canada's Wonderland, an amusement park north of Toronto. Her wages were modest, but they qualified as earned income for RRSP purposes. She's too young to open a TFSA, but she can contribute 18 percent of her earned income each year (the maximum allowed) to an RRSP. And she can defer claiming the tax deduction until she is working full-time and the deduction will be more worthwhile. Meanwhile, the money will be compounding inside her RRSP.

Let's say she earned $2800 over the summer. That will allow her to contribute $500 to an RRSP. She has 49 years before she reaches age 65. At an average annual growth rate of 5 percent, that $500 will grow more than 10 times, to $5460.67 at the end of that time. It's just one more example of the magic of compounding.

First-Time Homebuyers

One of the most popular features of RRSPs is the Home Buyers' Plan (HBP). This program allows first-time homebuyers to borrow up to $20,000 from an RRSP interest-free and to pay the money back over 15 years. Hundreds of thousands of Canadians have made use of it since the plan was introduced in 1992, originally as a temporary measure to help a beleaguered housing market. Now aspiring homeowners face the dilemma of whether to use an RRSP or a TFSA as the savings vehicle for their down payment.

An RRSP allows you to reach your financial goal more quickly because you do not pay tax on RRSP contributions (you get an offsetting tax deduction) and your money therefore accumulates faster. Take a look at the following chart. It shows how much money would be accumulated in each plan based on $3500 a year in before-tax income. I've assumed an annual rate of return of 5 percent and for purposes of the TFSA contribution, a marginal tax rate of 30 percent on the $3500.

Home Ownership Savings: TFSAs versus RRSPs

Year	RRSP	TFSA
1	$3675	$2573
2	$7534	$5274
3	$11,585	$8,110
4	$15,840	$11,088
5	$20,307	$14,215

At the end of five years, you will have accumulated more than $20,000 in the RRSP and can take maximum advantage of the HBP. The value of the TFSA, however, is only $14,215 because you were only able to contribute $2450 a year after tax. It will be almost another two years before the TFSA reaches the $20,000 level, by which time you'd have your house if you chose the RRSP.

If you had to withdraw the money outright from the RRSP to buy the home, it would be a different story because the $20,000 would be taxed coming out. But with the HBP (as well as the Lifelong Learning Plan, which allows interest-free RRSP loans for continuing education), no tax is assessed on withdrawals as long as the loan is repaid on schedule or faster.

So if saving for a first home is your number-one priority, the RRSP is the best way to do it. If you want to move even faster, use your RRSP refund to open a TFSA and save both ways.

Large Contributions

Because of the low contribution limits on TFSAs, big savers are better off using RRSPs because they can shelter more money from taxes. The maximum RRSP contribution for the 2009 tax year is

$21,000, more than four times the amount you can put into a TFSA.

Of course, you're allowed to do both—the two types of plans can be used in tandem to build a supersized retirement nest egg.

Action Summary

1. Contribute to an RRSP before a TFSA if you expect to be taxed at a lower rate after retirement. If your tax rate is likely to be higher than it is now, use the TFSA first.
2. If you are a member of a pension plan, contribute to TFSAs to supplement your retirement savings, especially if you have little or no RRSP room.
3. If you are planning to buy a house, save for your down payment in an RRSP rather than a TFSA and make use of the RRSP Home Buyers' Plan.

7

Some Shelter for Seniors

Although statistics tell us that many retired Canadians live below the poverty line, a lot of retirees are doing very well for themselves.

According to data published by the Canada Revenue Agency, about 4.3 million Canadians over age 65 filed tax returns for 2006 (the latest year for which figures were available at the time of writing). Of these, just over 2.3 million (54 percent) reported taxable income, in the amount of $120.5 billion. That works out to an average of about $52,000 per taxable filer.[1]

Let's consider the implications of those numbers. They suggest that almost half of older people (46 percent) live on incomes that are so low they don't even meet the minimum threshold for paying tax. In reality, the percentage is probably much higher because the data only covers tax filers. How many more seniors don't even bother to submit a return because their incomes are low or non-existent?

Compare that with the average income of tax-paying retirees and it's immediately apparent that there is a huge gap between the two groups. TFSAs don't bridge that chasm, although over time they may reduce the income disparity by giving lower-income people more incentive to save. But the first ones to benefit are those on the higher-income side of the retirement divide.

I frequently receive emails from older readers who are angry because the payments from their Registered Retirement Income Funds (RRIFs) are taxed at such a high rate (RRIFs are the programs used to generate income from RRSP savings). Some are so outraged, they say that if they had realized how much tax they'd have to pay they never would have bothered saving for retirement in the first place.

My response to such complaints is always the same: You're lucky. Anyone who has to pay high taxes does so because they enjoy above-average income. There are worse things to worry about in retirement than making too much money. I doubt many of the complainers would want to trade places with someone at the other end of the income scale.

That said, I understand the desire of these folks to cut their tax bills. And as long as it can be done legally, I encourage them to go ahead. TFSAs offer several ways to achieve that goal. The savings aren't necessarily dramatic, but every little bit helps.

Advance Planning

As we saw in the last chapter, anyone who expects their tax rate to be higher in retirement should be saving in a TFSA rather than an RRSP. There are a number of situations in which that might happen. Here are three examples:

You start a business. A growing number of people move on to a new career after they stop working. This may be anything from consulting to dog breeding. When combined with pension and investment income, the additional cash flow could push these people into a higher tax bracket.

Consider the example of a B.C. government worker with the provincial Ministry of Small Business and Revenue. Her pre-retirement income was $70,000, and her marginal tax rate was about 30 percent. She retires at 65 with a pension equal to 75 percent of her salary, or $52,500. She draws CPP benefits of $10,600 a year and Old Age Security of $6200, bringing the total to $69,300—almost as much as when she stopped working. She then decides to start a tax preparation service for small companies. It turns out to be highly successful and generates an additional in $25,000 net income. Her marginal tax rate has just jumped to more than 38 percent!

If this woman saved any money in an RRSP, she will have to pay more tax when it comes out than the value of the refund she received when she made the contribution. Had she put the same amount into a TFSA, she would end up ahead.

You receive a windfall. Everyone dreams of winning a lottery, but the most likely windfall you'll receive is an inheritance. As baby boomers approach retirement, many will lose their last surviving parent and the estate will pass to the next generation. Even after the government takes its tax cut, billions of dollars worth of savings, real estate, and insurance will end up in the hands of adult children who are themselves close to leaving the workforce.

In some cases, the inheritance may be worth hundreds of thousands of dollars or even more. When invested, this money will generate returns that, when added to other income, will move the heirs into higher tax brackets. To illustrate, a $500,000 inheritance that earns 6 percent a year will add $30,000 to a person's income. That's enough to push an Ontario resident who had been receiving $60,000 a year from a marginal tax rate of 31.15 percent all the way to 43.41 percent (2008 rates). While there won't be enough

TFSA room available for several years to shelter a large inheritance, anyone who anticipates receiving a bequest should open a plan now and be ready to move as much money as possible into it when the time comes.

You plan to move to a higher-tax province. Consider the case of a Nova Scotian who went to Alberta to work in the oil sands industry. He has made good money, slightly more than $100,000 a year. But because Alberta tax rates are so low, his marginal tax rate is only 36 percent. Now he's retiring and wants to return to Halifax where his family still lives. He'll receive less income in retirement—his pension, CPP, OAS, and a small amount of investment income will add up to about $87,000 a year. But because taxes are much higher in Nova Scotia, his marginal rate will actually rise to 42.67 percent.

In all these situations, starting a TFSA during the working years produces better post-retirement after-tax results than an RRSP.

After You've Retired

Even after you've fully retired, the TFSA/RRSP dilemma may still come into play. We are allowed to have RRSPs and to make contributions to them until the end of the year in which we turn 71. Even retirees with no earned income can take advantage of this situation if they have unused carry-forward room, which many do. Check your most recent Notice of Assessment from the Canada Revenue Agency to find out whether you do too. But is it worthwhile using this RRSP contribution room now that TFSAs are available?

Perhaps, but you need to look at the situation carefully. For starters, how much money is involved? You can contribute only

$5000 a year to a TFSA. If you have more than $5000 in unused RRSP contribution room and you have the necessary cash, you should make use of it. Remember, the more money you can tax-shelter and the sooner you can do it, the better.

Next, consider whether you expect your tax rate to be lower, higher, or about the same after age 71. If it is likely to be higher, forget about the RRSP unless you would rather exchange a small tax deduction now for a higher tax bill later. If you anticipate no change, it's a toss-up, but since you can only keep the RRSP for a few years longer anyway, you may want to go right to a TFSA.

You should also look at your exposure to the Old Age Security clawback, which cuts in when net income exceeds $64,781 (2008 rates). This onerous surtax grabs back 15 cents of every dollar of net income that exceeds the threshold. And that's on top of your regular tax rate. The effect is that a Quebec resident who receives OAS payments and has taxable income of $70,000 is being socked at a marginal rate of more than 53 percent! Since RRSP and RRIF payments count as income but TFSA withdrawals do not, anyone who expects to be subject to the clawback should opt for a TFSA.

For modest-income retirees (anyone earning less than $30,000 a year), it's a no-brainer. Choose the TFSA over an RRSP. This ensures you won't compromise your eligibility for the Guaranteed Income Supplement or various federal tax credits.

Most people over the age of 71 won't have to choose between a TFSA and an RRSP, but there are exceptions. Suppose a 72-year-old married woman (who can no longer hold an RRSP) has earned income and/or unused carry-forward room. Her disabled husband is 69 and is therefore still RRSP-eligible. In this case, the woman has a choice: She can make a contribution to a spousal RRSP or put money into a TFSA.

The key consideration here is what her husband's tax rate is likely to be in the future compared to her current marginal rate. In this case, the odds are that her husband's rate will be very low—in fact, he may not have to pay any tax at all once he claims the personal and disability credits. So the spousal RRSP would be the right choice—she gets a deduction now, and the money comes out of her husband's plan later as income in his hands. That means it will be taxed at a low rate or perhaps not at all.

RRIF/LIF Withdrawals

Once an RRSP is converted to an RRIF or a life income fund (LIF: a locked-in account funded by pension plan money), the federal government requires that a minimum amount be taken out of the plan annually. This is based on a percentage of the market value of the plan on January 1 of each year. The minimum percentage you are required to withdraw increases with age; at 70, it is 5 percent, but by the time you reach 75, it is up to 7.85 percent.

Canadians who have other sources of income, such as an employer pension, frequently complain that these forced withdrawals put them in a position of taking out more money than they need, thereby pushing them into a higher tax bracket. The tax implications are especially onerous in cases where RRIF/LIF withdrawals add enough to a person's income to move them over the OAS clawback threshold. The new pension-splitting rules may ease the tax situation for some couples, but most retirees would prefer to have greater flexibility in deciding how much to take out of a RRIF or LIF each year.

Two decades from now, TFSAs should have eased the problem because they allow future generations the flexibility to diversify their retirement savings, thereby reducing the dependence on taxable RRIFs. But what about today?

Unfortunately, TFSAs do nothing to ease the immediate tax bite of RRIF/LIF withdrawals. What they *can* do is to shelter future investment income from the tax folks.

Prior to TFSAs, there was no inexpensive tax-shelter program for Canadians over age 71. Universal life policies offer tax protection, but they are expensive, and if you don't already have one, your health may disqualify you. TFSAs change the landscape.

Retirees can now move $5000 a year (so $10,000 per couple) of unneeded RRIF/LIF withdrawals into TFSA accounts. Yes, they'll still pay tax on the money as it comes out of the RRIF/LIF, but at least they will be able to ensure they will not have to pay any more tax on the future investment income they earn.

Since older people have a shorter life expectancy, the benefits of TFSAs aren't as great as for people in their twenties. However, Statistics Canada tells us that a Canadian male aged between 70 and 74 can expect to live another 13.7 years, while a woman in the same age group can expect to survive another 16.7 years.[2]

So let's assume that a woman who is now age 70 starts contributing $5000 a year from unneeded RRIF withdrawals to a TFSA. She continues to do this for the next five years, during which time the investment income accrues at an average annual compound rate of 6 percent. By age 75, she has a tax-free nest egg worth $29,877. At this point, she finds that she needs the full amount of her RRIF withdrawal to live on, so she stops contributing her RRIF withdrawals to the TFSA and simply allows the money in the TFSA to continue compounding. By the time she is 80, the TFSA will be worth $39,982. At age 85, it will have grown to $53,504. At this point, her RRIF may be almost depleted, but she now has the TFSA to fall back on and she won't need to withdraw as much to live on because no tax will be withheld. If she doesn't need the money in the TFSA, it will make a nice inheritance for her children or grandchildren.

So even if you are in your seventies, don't ignore the tax-saving potential of these new plans. Sure, it would have been nice if they'd been available when you entered the workforce so many years ago, but better late than never.

Action Summary

1. If you are not yet retired, give careful thought to what your income is likely to be after you stop work and how much tax you will pay. It will help you decide whether to make any more RRSP contributions.
2. If you plan to move after you retire, check the tax rates in the province to which you are relocating.
3. Invest any unneeded RRIF withdrawal money in a TFSA, up to the annual limit.

8

TFSAs or RESPs?

Which type of savings plan should you choose for a child's or grandchild's college education? At first glance, there are a lot of similarities between Tax-Free Savings Accounts (TFSAs) and Registered Education Savings Plans (RESPs).

Both are funded with tax-paid money—you don't receive a deduction for your contributions.

Both tax-shelter investment income earned within the plan.

Both allow the tax-free withdrawal of contributions at any time.

Both have a contribution year-end of December 31, unlike RRSPs, which give you 60 days after the end of a calendar year to get your money into the plan.

But that's where the resemblance ends. RESPs come with several strings and conditions, as well as with government-sponsored savings incentives. TFSAs are much more flexible, but Ottawa doesn't kick in any extra cash to encourage you to use them.

So the answer is not as clear-cut as you might expect.

Registered Education Savings Plans (RESPs)

Let's begin by looking at the pros and cons of RESPs. These plans have been around for years but were seldom used until the federal government decided to give them a boost by creating the Canada Education Savings Grant (CESG). This is a program operated by Human Resources and Social Development Canada that adds a 20 percent bonus to your annual RESP contribution to a maximum of $500 a year (or $1000 if you have unused grant room from past years). The lifetime limit is $7200 per child and there are no income restrictions on these grants. They are paid directly into the RESP.

In addition, modest-income families get an extra grant on the first $500 they contribute to an RESP each year. This can be either 10 percent or 20 percent on $500—in other words, $50 or $100 on top of the basic grant. The lower the income, the greater the amount, although families with net income as high as about $75,000 can qualify for this extra grant. The qualifying net income of the child's family for a year will generally be the same as the income used to determine eligibility for the Canada Child Tax Benefit.

These grants are paid until the year the child (technically known as the "plan beneficiary") turns 17. But there are some conditions. Grants will only be paid on behalf of beneficiaries who are 16 or 17 if the RESP was set up before they turned 16 and a minimum of $100 a year was contributed to the plan for four years. The other option is to put at least $2000 into the plan before the beneficiary turns age 16 (which could all be contributed in a single year or spread out).

What this boils down to is that for older children to qualify for the CESG, the RESP must be set up before the end of the calendar year in which the child turns 15 and the required contributions must be made.

The CESG is a powerful incentive to use RESPs and can add thousands of dollars to the end value of a plan. For example, suppose a parent opens an RESP for a newborn and contributes enough money each year to earn the basic grant. In the child's 15th year, the maximum lifetime grant of $7200 will be reached. If the money in the RESP earns 6 percent annually, by the time the child is 18, the added value of the CESG plus accumulated earnings will be more than $14,000.

There's more! Families who are entitled to the National Child Benefit (NCB) may qualify for up to $2000 in additional government incentives through what is known as the Canada Learning Bond (CLB). This provides an additional $500 for children born in 2004 or later, plus $25 in the first year to help pay for the cost of setting up an RESP. After that, an additional $100 a year will be deposited into the RESP for up to 15 years as long as the family qualifies for the NCB.

No wonder RESPs have become more popular in recent years!

Another advantage offered by these plans is contribution flexibility. In the past, parents or grandparents were restricted to a maximum annual contribution of $4000. Now there is no annual maximum—the only limitation is that the lifetime amount contributed on behalf of any one child cannot exceed $50,000. (Remember, however, that only the first $2500 contributed qualifies for the CESG in that year.) You are allowed to make contributions until the plan beneficiary turns 31.

Now let's consider the drawbacks of RESPs.

Income taxed on withdrawal. Although contributions to an RESP can be withdrawn tax-free at any time, investment income earned within a plan is taxed when it comes out. These are called educational assistance payments (EAPs). Fortunately, such withdrawals are deemed to be income received by the student, not the contributor. Since a college student is likely to have limited income from other sources, tax payable on RESP withdrawals may not be significant indeed, the student may have no taxable income at all once the tuition and education tax credits are applied.

Money must be used for education. The rules governing RESP withdrawals are fairly loose. As long as the end use relates to post-secondary education, almost anything goes. Withdrawals can be used to pay for tuition, residence, books, travel, athletics, even a computer. And there is nothing in the rules that says the beneficiary must go to a Canadian college; an RESP can be used to finance a Harvard education if the student can gain admission. But if the beneficiary does not go on to post-secondary studies, there's a problem. This is where the real downside of RESPs comes into play.

Penalties if a child quits school. The major risk of RESPs is the extremely high tax penalty that contributors face if the plan beneficiary decides not to pursue a post-secondary education. These plans are specifically intended for education saving, and the government hits contributors with hefty taxes if things don't work out that way (most RESPs must be wound up by their 35th-anniversary date).

You might argue that this is inherently unfair. After all, it is not the fault of the parents if their daughter decides that college isn't her thing or if her marks aren't good enough to gain admission.

They did everything they were supposed to, dutifully cutting back their spending so they could put money aside for her schooling. Why should they be penalized when she decides she would rather take a job at the local mall or travel around the world? After all, the government doesn't punish RRSP investors if they don't use the money to fund their retirement.

If a child decides not to go on to post-secondary education, the cost to the plan and the contributor can amount to thousands of dollars. The contributor may withdraw the contributions tax-free but will have to repay all the money received from the Canada Education Savings Grant and the Canada Learning Bond to the government.

The money that remains in the RESP will consist of the investment income earned over the years. In a case where $2500 a year was contributed to a plan over 18 years that earned 6 percent annually, the investment earnings will amount to almost $37,000.

Once the contributor takes this money out of an RESP that is not used by the beneficiary, it is called an accumulated income payment (AIP). If the contributing parent or grandparent has an RRSP and enough contribution room available, he or she can move the AIP there directly without having to pay tax on it (or use a spousal plan). But if an RRSP transfer is not feasible, the tax hit is fierce.

In that case, the AIP will be added to your regular income for the year in which it is received. That means it will be taxed at your marginal rate. But the government wants more. You'll be hit with an extra 20 percent penalty on top of that (12 percent in Quebec), which pushes the effective tax rate to almost confiscatory levels.

To put this in perspective, let's look at the case of an Ontario father who has a taxable income of $60,000 a year. The family scrimped and saved in an RESP to send their son (an only child) to university, but he was academically challenged and dropped out of high school in his senior year. The parents were not only disappointed with his decision but were left with the problem of winding up the RESP. After repaying the government grants and withdrawing their principal, the RESP had $25,000 remaining in it. Since neither parent had any RRSP contribution room available, the money had to be withdrawn as an AIP.

Based on 2008 rates, the normal tax payable on the $25,000 withdrawal would be $9277, based on the father's regular income. But the 20 percent penalty would add $5000 to the bill, bringing the total to $14,277. That works out to an effective tax rate of 57.1 percent on the AIP. There is no reasonable justification for this, but it is how the system operates. The result is that RESPs are something of a gamble, despite all the government support.

Scholarship trusts. There is one other risk to RESPs that relates directly to the type of plan used. Scholarship trusts have aggressively marketed RESP programs for years, and some have been quite successful. Students who meet the qualifications and use the plans to go through college can receive generous grants.

But the trusts charge hefty up-front fees, and families that decide to drop out of the plan early can end up losing thousands of dollars. So they carry a double risk—first, that the child may not go on to college and second, that the parents may not be able to keep up with the payment schedule.

Tax-Free Savings Accounts and Education Savings

There are no bells and whistles if you decide to use a TFSA rather than an RESP to save for a child's education. You get no government support—the only money in the plan is what you contribute.

But there is also no risk. The money that accumulates in a TFSA can be used for any purpose at all. The government won't sock it to you if your child or grandchild decides not to go to university.

This flexibility means that there is no pressure on a child to do something he or she doesn't want to do. It also means that the money you've accumulated can be used for some other purpose, such as providing a down payment on a first home or paying for a wedding.

What makes the decision so difficult is that there is no way of knowing when a child is young whether that child will eventually go on to post-secondary education. Surprisingly, there appears to be no data that tells us what percentage of children in Canada who start elementary school eventually proceed to some form of post-secondary education. When I put that question to the Ontario Ministry of Education, I was informed by a researcher that "the requested data will be available starting 2017–2018 as the ministry started collecting elementary student level data in 2005–2006 school year for the first time." That's not much help to a parent who is trying to decide right now whether to risk opening an RESP.

A report published in 2006 by Colleges Ontario found that 52 percent of Ontario high school graduates enrolled in college or university.[1] However, this only refers to students who actually finished high school.

If the federal government were to eliminate the 20 percent tax penalty, parents would not be faced with such a difficult choice. But unless that happens, Canadians will be forced to make a decision when a child is very young that they may come to regret years later.

From a strictly financial perspective, an RESP is the better choice if the plan beneficiary is young. The following table compares the value of an RESP and a TFSA at the end of various time frames. It assumes an annual contribution of $2500 plus the payment of the basic CESG to the RESP at a rate of $500 a year to a maximum of $7200. The average annual compound rate of return is 6 percent.

RESPs versus TFSAs (1)

Years	TFSA	RESP	RESP gain
5	$14,938	$17,926	+$2988
10	$34,929	$41,915	+$6986
15	$61,681	$73,700	+$12,019
20	$97,482	$113,565	+$16,083

Assumption: Average annual compound rate of return is 6%.

As you can see, the RESP offers a significant financial advantage, and the longer the plan is in existence, the greater the differential. However, the only reason the RESP generates more money is the contribution from the Canada Education Savings Grant. Without the CESG, the end result for both plans would be the same.

But remember, if a child does not have an RESP opened for her before the end of the year she turns 15, she will not be eligible for the CESG. This changes the equation for people who come late to education savings. With the CESG removed from the calculation, the advantage shifts to using a TFSA rather than an RESP for the following reasons:

Same financial result. Both plans will accumulate the same amount of money, assuming equal contributions and rates of return.

No withdrawal restrictions. TFSA savings don't have to be used for education purposes. If the child decides not to go to college, the money can be spent on something else or simply left in the plan to accumulate.

No tax on withdrawals. Although the tax rate on most RESP withdrawals will be low or non-existent, TFSA withdrawals are completely tax-free.

However, keep in mind that only $5000 a year can be contributed to a TFSA, whereas there is no annual limit on RESPs. If the goal is to quickly build a large education fund for an older child who is certain to go on to post-secondary education, consider using the two plans in combination.

A TFSA may also be a better choice for people with a lot of money. If the parent or grandparent wants to contribute more than $50,000 to an education savings plan (the maximum allowed per child in an RESP) and the contributions are spread over several years, a TFSA produces a better return in the end.

Let's look at a scenario of a child born in 2009. The parents want to save $5000 a year for her education. Which plan works better? After 10 years, the lifetime RESP maximum is reached and the contributions stop. But since there is no such restriction on TFSAs, the payments continue.

The RESP receives the maximum $500 grant each year for a total of $5000. (Since there is no accumulated grant room, the parents lose out on the remaining $2200 of CESG payments.) Here is the result.

RESPs versus TFSAs (2)

Years	TFSA	RESP	RESP gain/loss
5	$29,877	$32,864	+$2987
10	$69,858	$76,844	+$6986
15	$123,363	$102,835	-$20,528
20	$194,964	$137,616	-$57,348

Assumption: Average annual compound rate of return is 6%.

Thanks to the accelerated CESG payment, the RESP jumps into an early lead. But after year 10, when RESP contributions cease, the TFSA starts to close the gap. At the end of year 12, the value of both plans is almost equal. After that, the TFSA moves ahead and the gap continues to widen in each subsequent year.

However, keep in mind that twice as much money is contributed by the parents or grandparents to the TFSA as to the RESP. The RESP is actually more efficient because of the CESG, even though the amount of money in the plan after 20 years is $50,000 less.

The bottom line is that if the child is eligible for the Canada Education Savings Grant, an RESP is a more efficient way to save for college from a financial perspective. But each family will have to decide whether it is willing to live with the tax risk involved if the student does not choose to pursue post-secondary education.

Action Summary

1. For young children, open an RESP instead of a TFSA for education savings because of the added benefit of the CESG.

However, be aware of the potential tax risk if the child does not go on to post-secondary education.

2. For older children who do not already have RESPs, use a TFSA to save for their education unless you anticipate making contributions of more than $5000 a year.

9

A New Way to Split Income

The Government of Canada has never liked the concept of income splitting, perhaps because it would cost the federal Treasury too much in lost revenue. This means that Canadian couples end up paying a lot more in taxes than, for example, American couples, who are allowed to file joint returns.

The extra tax we pay can add up to thousands of dollars a year per couple. Take a look at the following table. It shows how much money could be saved in taxes each year by Ontario couples of various income levels if full income splitting were allowed in Canada, assuming both were earning the same amount. The figures are based on 2008 tax rates. I used the online Personal Tax Calculator provided by the accounting firm of Ernst & Young to crunch the numbers.[1]

The table clearly illustrates that if couples were allowed to file joint tax returns, the savings would be significant. Moreover, the last column shows that such a change in policy would provide the greatest relief to lower-income families, leaving them with more

The Effect of Income Splitting

Family taxable income	Tax (current system)	Tax (income splitting)	Savings	Tax reduction
$30,000	$4350	$2344	$2006	46.1%
$40,000	$6726	$4490	$2236	33.2%
$50,000	$9841	$6594	$3247	33.0%
$60,000	$12,956	$8700	$4256	32.8%
$80,000	$20,062	$13,452	$6610	32.9%
$100,000	$28,744	$19,682	$9062	31.5%
$150,000	$51,254	$35,846	$15,408	30.1%

after-tax income. In some cases, this might be enough to remove them from social welfare rolls.

The Conservative Party has dabbled with income splitting, which suggests that we may be slowly moving in that direction. In 2007, new rules took effect that allowed pension income to be divided between spouses or partners. However, the regulations make the program so complicated that even tax professionals had trouble figuring out the optimum split in individual situations in its first year.

The Conservative Party's 2008 election platform contained a promise to extend income splitting to caregivers of family members with disabilities. But that would apply to only a small number of people. For the great majority of Canadians, income splitting remains an elusive dream.

In addition to limiting income splitting to just a few situations, the Canada Revenue Agency has strict rules that prevent the transfer of assets from one spouse to another (or to minor children) for purposes of dividing investment income. Under these "income attribution" regulations, any dividends, capital gains, or interest earned in this way must be declared for tax purposes by the person who provided the money originally.

For example, suppose a husband wanted to give $50,000 to his wife as a gift. The transfer of money in itself is not illegal and does not attract tax. But now let's assume the wife invests the cash and earns 5 percent on it, which works out to $2500 in the first year. That income must be declared on the husband's tax return, not hers.

TFSAs are a game changer. It will take time, but over several years, a couple can put together a meaningful income-splitting plan, at least as far as their investments are concerned.

The key that makes this possible is that the Canada Revenue Agency waives the attribution rules when the money is used to invest in a TFSA. Annex 4 of the 2008 Budget Plan states:

> If an individual transfers property to the individual's spouse or common-law partner, the income tax rules generally treat any income earned on that property as income of the individual. An exception to these "attribution rules" will allow individuals to take advantage of the TFSA contribution room available to them using funds provided by their spouse or common-law partner: the rules will not apply to income earned in a TFSA that is derived from such contributions.[2]

This means that even if a wife has no income and no assets, the husband can transfer up to $5000 a year to her (based on the initial contribution limit) to invest in a TFSA. As her plan builds, the effect will be to effectively switch investment income from his hands to hers for tax purposes.

Over a period of 10 years, this strategy would shift $50,000 in capital from the husband to the wife. Assuming an average annual return of 6 percent, the value of the wife's TFSA at the end of that time will be $67,852. Let's also assume the husband's income is $85,000 a year. Using TFSAs works out to a tax saving for the husband of $5429.[3] The figure is based on an investment in a diversified portfolio in which the investment earnings are 40 percent interest, 30 percent dividends, and 30 percent capital gains.

People with more modest incomes won't save quite as much because they will be in a lower tax bracket. But even if the husband only earns $45,000 a year, the cumulative tax saving would be almost $4300.

The greatest beneficiaries will be young people because the longer the time frame, the more investment income is earned in the plan and the greater the tax savings.

Let's consider the case of a couple who are both 30 years old and who adopt twin girls. They decide that the husband will be a stay-at-home dad while the wife remains on in her well-paying job as a human resources manager for a medium-sized oil company where she earns $105,000 annually.

In order to move some income into his hands, she gives her husband $5000 a year to invest in a TFSA. He is quite knowledgeable about investing and succeeds in generating an average annual return of 8 percent over the years. Assuming her income stays constant and tax rates don't change (which of course they will, but this is an illustration), the amount of tax saved over 30 years will be a whopping $193,240. And that's just the tax they've kept in their own hands! The total value of his TFSA at the end of that time will be $588,637.

The tax savings would be exactly the same if the wife had simply opened her own TFSA account instead. However, this strategy gives the couple double the tax-saving power. If she makes the same contributions to her own TFSA and achieves similar returns, their combined tax savings after 30 years is $386,480!

Of course, this couple's financial position would be even better if full income splitting were allowed. But for now, this is a pretty good start.

Action Summary

1. Use TFSAs to split investment income between you and your spouse, potentially saving you thousands of tax dollars over the years.
2. Get your spouse to open a plan as well, to double the tax-saving potential.

10

Leaving More for the Kids

I receive dozens of emails each year from older people asking about how they can leave more money to their children and grandchildren when they pass on.

There are ways to achieve this, but they typically involve complex legal structures, such as trusts, and they can be costly. Unless there is a great deal of money involved, it may not be worth the time and expense.

In some ways, Canadians are better off than our neighbours to the south when it comes to passing on assets to the next generation. The United States imposes hefty succession taxes on its well-to-do citizens. Right now, these are being reduced, but the tax rates will revert to previous levels in 2011 unless Congress moves to abolish them permanently. Given the current state of the U.S. Treasury, that does not seem likely.

We have no estate tax as such in Canada. However, our governments have figured out other ways to grab a large chunk of your money when you die that can be almost as onerous.

This happens when the wealth transfer is to the next generation. Your assets can pass to your spouse or common-law partner after your death with no tax implications. The big hit occurs when the last surviving spouse or partner dies and the estate is transferred to the children or other heirs. For most families, the tax bite at this stage occurs in two ways.

Crystallizing of capital gains at death. When you die, all your investments are deemed to have been sold at fair market value. This means that any profits you have on stocks, mutual funds, real property (other than the principal residence), bonds, and so forth are treated as taxable capital gains on your final tax return. (Yes, the government requires that you, or more precisely, your estate, file a tax return even after you are dead.)

Closing of all registered plans. Any RRSPs, RRIFs, LIFs, and such that you own are considered to have been terminated on the day you die. All the money in the accounts is treated as personal income on your final tax return.

This can result in a huge tax bill because all this extra income will attract the top marginal rate, which in some provinces is more than 48 percent. The following table shows how much tax will be assessed on a final return depending on where in Canada the deceased lived and on the taxable value of the estate. The figures are based on 2008 tax rates and are provided by the Ernst & Young online Personal Tax Calculator. They do not include provincial probate fees.

One thing this table tells us is that the best way to minimize tax on your estate is to be a resident of Alberta or Nunavut when you die. Try to avoid dying in Quebec or Nova Scotia, both of which really sock it to the dearly departed.

Death Taxes in Canada

Domicile	$100,000	$250,000	$500,000	$750,000	$1,000,000
British Columbia	$26,579	$91,433	$200,683	$309,933	$419,183
Alberta	$27,261	$85,065	$182,565	$280,065	$377,565
Saskatchewan	$30,111	$95,179	$205,179	$315,179	$425,179
Manitoba	$31,767	$100,671	$216,671	$332,671	$448,671
Ontario	$28,744	$97,664	$213,689	$329,714	$445,739
Quebec	$33,220	$104,967	$225,517	$346,067	$466,617
New Brunswick	$32,040	$101,617	$218,992	$336,367	$453,742
Nova Scotia	$32,613	$104,292	$224,917	$345,542	$466,167
Prince Edward Island	$31,718	$102,077	$220,502	$338,927	$457,352
Newfoundland and Labrador	$31,084	$97,889	$210,389	$322,889	$435,389
Northwest Territories	$26,785	$90,350	$197,975	$305,600	$413,225
Yukon	$27,429	$90,012	$196,012	$302,012	$408,012
Nunavut	$24,771	$84,245	$185,495	$286,745	$387,995

Even on a relatively modest $100,000 estate (taxable income), the heirs of a deceased Quebecer will inherit $8449 less than those of someone who dies in Nunavut. On large estates, the tax gap becomes tens of thousands of dollars. The heirs of a Nova Scotia resident with a million-dollar estate will end up with $88,602 less than the survivors of a person who passes away in Alberta leaving behind the same amount. So anyone from Down East who left home to work in the oil fields won't do his family any favours by going back to Nova Scotia to die.

TFSAs and Estate Planning

The creation of TFSAs changes the estate planning ground rules. That's because money accumulated in these plans does not attract any tax at death.

Therefore, one of the first priorities of older people who want to maximize the after-tax value of their estates should be to move as much money as possible from non-registered investment accounts into TFSAs.

For example, let's assume a couple who are both 70 years old has $50,000 invested in non-registered accounts. Of this, $30,000 is in the wife's name and is invested in blue-chip stocks. The husband has the other $20,000 invested in GICs. They have two children to whom they want to leave equal shares of the estate.

Looking at this situation strictly from an estate planning perspective, the GICs will attract little tax at death, since they have no capital gains potential. Only the interest earned will be taxed. The stocks are another matter. The wife's portfolio took a beating in the market collapse of autumn 2008, and every stock in it is currently in a loss position. However, when the markets rebound, she expects the stocks to quickly move back into profit territory. How should they proceed?

First, they should both open TFSA accounts immediately. Next, the wife should sell $10,000 worth of her money-losing securities. With the proceeds, she should contribute $5000 to her own TFSA and give her husband the other $5000 for his plan. Remember, it is important that she not contribute the losing stocks directly to a TFSA. If she makes a contribution in kind, the loss will not be allowed for tax purposes (but any capital gain triggered in such circumstances will be taxable). By selling them in the market, though, she triggers a capital loss that can be deducted from past, current, or future capital gains.

From a pure tax planning perspective, this is not necessarily the best course of action because the interest earned on the husband's GIC is taxed at his marginal rate, whereas dividends and capital gains get a break. But the point of this exercise is to protect the children's inheritance from the taxman. If the couple uses the cash in the TFSAs to buy new stocks that appreciate in value, the capital gains will not be taxed when they die.

The couple should repeat this process each year until all of the wife's assets have been moved into the TFSAs. After that, the husband's GIC assets can be switched over in the same way. The GICs do not have to be sold first; they can go into the TFSA directly as a contribution in kind. At the end of five years, the couple's entire non-registered portfolio will be safe from taxation when they die.

RRSP/RRIF Strategies

A similar strategy could be considered with RRSPs and RRIFs, although the fact that any money withdrawn from these plans is taxable immediately makes the decision more complicated. In this situation, the current tax status of the plan holder is a major factor. If the person is in a low tax bracket, taking out an after-tax amount of $5000 a year and moving it into a TFSA may reduce the total tax bite on those savings at death. Let's look at the case of a B.C. man who is 70 years old and has $100,000 in a RRIF. He is a widower and plans to leave his estate to his only daughter. His annual taxable income is $32,000, which means his marginal tax rate is 20.24 percent (2008 rates). If he were to die at the end of this year, the $100,000 in the RRIF would be added to his income, increasing the total to $132,000 for purposes of his final tax return. The extra tax on the RRIF money would add $35,312 to the assessment, a tax rate of 35.31 percent. So his daughter would inherit only $64,688 of the proceeds of the RRIF after tax.

If the father withdraws an extra $6275 from his RRIF this year, he will be assessed $1270 tax on the payment, leaving him with just over $5,000 after tax. He can then open a TFSA and deposit the money, repeating the same process each year. Essentially, he is paying tax at a lower rate now than would be assessed on the RRIF if he dies. After the money goes into the TFSA, it grows tax-free, and no tax will be assessed on the plan's value at the time of his death.

This strategy is not a guaranteed financial winner because if the father lives long enough, the value of the RRIF may be reduced to the point where the tax assessed at death will be very low anyway. Moreover, by paying tax on the extra withdrawals early, he loses the investment income that this tax money could have earned if it had remained in the RRIF. Over five years, assuming annual compounding of 6 percent, $1270 will generate about $430 in investment income.

Although it does not apply in this illustration, people 65 or older with higher income need to consider whether extra RRIF or RRSP withdrawals will push them over the Old Age Security clawback threshold, thereby raising their effective tax rate. That would change the entire equation.

You will need to carefully analyze your particular situation before you take any action. If there is a large amount of money involved, consult a financial professional before embarking on this strategy.

The Fine Print

There is some fine print that people need to be aware of when considering the estate-planning aspects of a TFSA, as well as some still-unanswered questions.

When the program was originally announced, the government said that a TFSA would cease being a tax shelter when the plan owner died. Annex 4 of the 2008 Budget Plan states:

> Generally, an individual's TFSA will lose its tax-exempt status upon the death of the individual. (That is, investment income and gains that accrue in the account after the individual's death will be taxable, while those that accrued before death will remain exempt.) However, an individual will be permitted to name his or her spouse or common-law partner as the successor account holder, in which case the account will maintain its tax-exempt status. Alternatively, the assets of a deceased individual's TFSA may be transferred to a TFSA of the surviving spouse or common-law partner, regardless of whether the survivor has available contribution room, and without reducing the survivor's existing room.[1]

Let's break this down. If there is a surviving spouse or partner, the assets in a TFSA can pass directly to that person. The easiest way to do this is to name the spouse as the "successor account holder." You can do this on the application form you complete when you first set up a plan.

If you don't name your spouse as the successor account holder, the money in the plan can still be transferred to his or her account without tax consequences and without reducing the spouse's personal contribution room. This can be done if the survivor has been named as the beneficiary. However, the designation of a beneficiary is governed by provincial succession laws and at the time of writing any changes were still under consideration. The amount that can be transferred in this case—called the "exempt contribution"—is limited to the fair market value of the TFSA at the time of death. So for now, be sure to make a successor account holder designation when the plan is created.

The original proposal contained in the budget said that a TFSA would effectively be de-registered and lose its tax-exempt status when the plan holder dies. That raised red flags with tax experts, who warned that it could create problems in situations where the plan administrator was not notified of the death for weeks or even months after the fact.

The Department of Finance responded to these concerns by proposing changes to the rules to allow for more flexibility and to avoid "causing undue administrative and reporting difficulties." These amendments were tabled in the House of Commons in July 2008.[2] They were intended to bring the tax treatment of TFSAs after death more closely in line with the rules governing RRSPs. However, the amendments died on the order paper when the October election was called. They are expected to be reintroduced in the new parliamentary session.

The main proposed change allows TFSAs to retain their tax-exempt status until the end of the year following the year of the plan holder's death. So if a TFSA investor dies in 2011, the plan will keep its tax-exempt status until December 31, 2012. After that, it loses its TFSA status and becomes a plain, non-registered investment account. If that happens, every security in the portfolio will be assigned a fair market value, and any interest, dividends, or capital gains earned after that will be taxed at normal rates.

Let's consider some of the scenarios that can arise on the death of a TFSA plan holder.

1. The spouse or partner is named as the successor account holder. In this case, the assets in the deceased person's TFSA are transferred directly into the TFSA of the survivor. That

person retains the contribution room he or she previously had; the transfer has no effect on that. In effect, the survivor simply steps into the shoes of the deceased.

2. The spouse or partner is named as beneficiary but not as successor account holder. The situation becomes more complicated in this case. The TFSA retains its tax-exempt status at death, but the amount that can come out of the plan tax-free is frozen at the market value on the day the plan holder died. Any investment income earned after that time is taxed at normal rates in the hands of the beneficiary.

   For example, let's assume a husband dies and leaves behind a TFSA worth $100,000. Over the next six months, the value of the plan increases to $120,000. At that point, the estate is settled and the assets in the TFSA pass to the wife. She can then transfer $100,000 tax-free to her own TFSA. However, the remaining $20,000 will be treated as taxable income when she files her return for that year and will be taxed at her marginal rate.

3. The last surviving spouse or partner dies and the TFSA passes to the next generation. For purposes of this example, we'll assume it is to be divided between two children, an adult brother and sister.

   In this case, the $100,000 in the plan at the time of death remains tax-free, but it cannot be transferred directly to the children's TFSAs unless they have adequate contribution room available. The $20,000 earned after death is taxable as income in their hands.

   But here is an angle that will likely become increasingly important in estate planning. The executor has the flexibility to decide how the TFSA assets are divided and can use that discretion to minimize the tax due on the $20,000.

Let's say that the brother is unemployed and therefore has very little income. The sister is a vice-president of a large company and is in the top tax bracket. As the legislation is currently worded, the executor can direct that the sister's share of the $120,000 in the TFSA be received as a $60,000 tax-exempt transfer. The brother receives $40,000 in tax-exempt money and $20,000 in taxable income. Since he is in a very low bracket, the amount of tax he will actually end up paying will be minimal. (This is a loophole that may be closed in the future, so estate planners will need to keep watch on the situation.)

4. The status of the TFSA is not resolved by the end of the year following death. This will be a rare occurrence, but if it happens, the rules state that the TFSA becomes a taxable trust. The $100,000 that was in the plan at the time of death retains tax-exempt status. The $20,000 earned in the plan after death becomes taxable at trust rates. This status will continue until such time as the trust is liquidated.

There is another complicating factor that will probably take some time to resolve, perhaps years. That is the question of whether the assets in a TFSA are subject to probate. It's an important point for two reasons. First, if a TFSA must go through probate, it is considered part of the estate; it may be many months before the beneficiaries can access the money. Second, several provinces, notably Ontario, British Columbia, and Nova Scotia, have greatly increased their probate fees in recent years. The fees are assessed as a percentage of the total value of the estate, which means that if a TFSA is included, the cost will be higher.

RRIFs, RRSPs, and other registered plans are exempt from probate in most of Canada. However, as of the time of writing, no province had taken the steps needed to add TFSAs to the list.

The Ontario Bar Association and the Investment Funds Institute of Canada are actively lobbying the Ontario government to bring in changes to the province's Succession Law Reform Act to make TFSAs exempt from probate. "It's the last piece of the TFSA puzzle," says Sandy Cardy, vice-president of Tax and Estate Planning Services for Mackenzie Financial.

It is expected that the Ontario law will eventually be changed and that other provinces will follow suit, but at this time, there is no way of knowing how long that will take.

There is no standardized form for setting up a TFSA, so be sure to review the application you are given carefully. Make sure that it allows you to designate a successor account holder, as allowed by federal law. It is recommended that everyone who has a spouse or common-law partner take advantage of this provision. It will not eliminate the probate requirement until the provincial rules are changed, but it will simplify the process of transferring the TFSA assets to the surviving spouse.

Also, check to see whether the form allows you to name a beneficiary. That way, if provincial succession laws are changed in the future, you won't have to fill out a new application or an amendment.

If there is no area on the form for making these designations, ask that they be written in.

Action Summary

1. Move assets from non-registered accounts into TFSAs to reduce tax at death.

2. Begin with securities that are likely to appreciate most in value.
3. Consult a financial professional before deciding whether to make early withdrawals from an RRSP or RRIF in order to make TFSA contributions.
4. Name your spouse or partner as the successor account holder when you first set up a TFSA. Also, to cover all the bases, designate a beneficiary as well.
5. As an extra safeguard, designate the person who is to receive your TFSA assets in your will.
6. When TFSA assets pass to the next generation, the executor of the estate should ensure they are distributed in the most tax-efficient manner.

11

Tax-Saving Strategies

As we have already seen, there are many ways to save taxes by using TFSAs. However, we have only scratched the surface. As the program becomes well established, astute accountants and financial planners will undoubtedly come up with many more ideas, although some may be complex.

In this chapter, let's look at some easy-to-implement tax-saving strategies that we have not yet examined in depth.

Choose the Right Securities

In order to maximize the tax efficiency of your TFSA, it is essential that you choose the right securities for the plan. If you're earning a return of only 2 percent, which is what Canada Savings Bonds were paying in the fall of 2008, it's hardly worth the effort to open a plan.

With RRSPs, the conventional wisdom is to hold interest-paying securities, such as bonds and GICs, inside the registered plan while keeping dividend-paying investments and growth stocks in a non-registered account. The logic for this is simple. All income drawn from an RRSP (or a RRIF/LIF) is taxed at your marginal rate, regardless of its original source. This means that interest, dividends, capital gains, and even return of capital are all taxed exactly the same when the money is earned inside a registered plan.

In the real world of non-registered accounts, the tax treatment is much different. Dividends are eligible for the dividend tax credit, which dramatically cuts the rate you actually pay. For example, a Saskatchewan resident with taxable income of $45,000 pays a marginal rate of 35 percent on RRSP or RRIF withdrawals. But the tax rate on dividends from public companies received in a non-registered account is only 7.3 percent. Clearly, it makes sense in this particular case to keep those dividend-paying stocks outside an RRSP if at all possible.

The same is true of any investments that have been purchased with a view to generating capital gains, such as stocks and equity mutual funds. If these securities are held in a non-registered account, only 50 percent of any gain is taxable, and gains can be offset by capital losses. But all capital gains earned in RRSPs and RRIFs will be taxed at your marginal rate when they come out and, to make matters worse, you can't claim any capital losses.

Certain types of securities also produce what is known as return of capital (ROC), which is not taxable in the year it is received. Income that is deemed to be ROC is deducted from the price you originally paid for the security, creating what is called an adjusted cost base (ACB). The ACB is eventually used to calculate any capital gain or loss when the security is sold. The net effect is that you benefit from tax sheltering until you sell, at which time you are taxed at the capital gains rate.[1]

A number of mutual fund companies offer products that make some or all of their distributions in the form of return of capital. But if you hold these inside an RRSP, all this clever tax-saving manipulation is lost.

TFSAs require a change in thinking. Since no taxes are assessed when money comes out of the plan, the RRSP tax planning strategies don't apply. You need to take a different approach if you are going to maximize the tax-free effectiveness of a TFSA.

A Capital Gains Strategy

In their 2006 campaign platform, the federal Conservatives promised to exempt capital gains from tax if the proceeds were reinvested within six months. They never delivered on that pledge, but TFSAs could have the long-term effect of making most capital gains tax-free. (There will be exceptions, such as a vacation property, because direct ownership of real estate within these plans is not permitted.)

So while it is true that capital gains receive a good break when they are earned outside a registered plan, they get even better treatment within a TFSA. Instead of paying tax on half of your profits, you get to keep the whole amount. The only downside is that you can't deduct capital losses incurred within a TFSA against gains made outside a plan.

Focusing a TFSA on capital gains looks even more attractive when we take another look at the contribution rules. Remember that any withdrawals from a plan are added back to your contribution limit in future years. So if you are smart or lucky (or both), you may be able to build your TFSA much faster than you might expect.

Let's consider a scenario that, while hypothetical, is certainly feasible. In the fall of 2008, world stock markets crashed. The S&P/TSX Composite Index lost 40 percent from early June to early October. At the time of writing, we do not know where the bottom is or how long the bear market will last. What history does tell us, however, is that when stock markets shift into recovery mode, the gains can be dramatic.

The high-tech collapse that opened this century provides a good example. Between the late winter of 2000 and October 2002, stock markets dived, led down by NASDAQ, which eventually lost about 80 percent of its value. But after a final huge sell-off in September and October 2002 (technically known as the "capitulation" stage in a market collapse), a rally began. Between December 31, 2002, and June 6, 2008, the S&P/TSX Composite Index rose from 8221 to 15,155—a gain of 84 percent.

Many blue-chip stocks doubled, tripled, even quadrupled in value during that period. At one point during the 2002 sell-off, you could have bought shares in TD Bank for as low as $25.17. In November 2007, you could have sold them for as much as $75, a profit of almost 200 percent.

Resource stocks fared even better. The shares of Potash Corporation of Saskatchewan traded as low as $13.23 during 2002. In June 2008, they touched a high of $246.29, an astounding gain of more than 1700 percent!

It's unrealistic to expect to pick winners of that magnitude on a consistent basis. What is *not* unrealistic is the possibility—indeed the probability—that high-quality stocks will double in value in the two to three years following the end of a deep bear market.

Here is a capital gains strategy that flows from that thinking. Open a TFSA now and invest the $5000 yearly contribution limit in two or three quality stocks. Choose companies that are industry leaders and have a well-established history of surviving even the toughest times. Do the same thing at the start of year two, which will give you a total investment of $10,000.

If the scenario plays out as predicted, by the end of the second year, your TFSA stands a good chance of doubling in value. You now have $20,000 in the plan. You decide to sell the stocks and withdraw the cash to use for the down payment on a rental property. There are no capital gains taxes to pay.

In the next year, your contribution room will increase to $25,000—the $5000 basic entitlement plus the $20,000 you withdrew. Now you can begin the process of rebuilding the TFSA to the extent that your financial resources permit. The net result is that you now own an income property plus you have increased the amount of money you can shelter from tax in the future.

Of course, the timing has to be right, you must have the temperament to accept stock market risk, and you must choose the right companies for this to work. But it is a strategy worth considering, especially coming out of a bear market.

A Dividend Strategy

At first glance, it would seem that the capital gains strategy I have described would also apply to dividends. Yes, they get a tax advantage in a non-registered account, but you pay no tax at all if they are earned in a TFSA.

But here's the wrinkle. If your taxable income is relatively low and you invest in dividend stocks with little or no growth potential (preferred shares are a classic example), you may decide to use the TFSA for something else.

There are some quirks to the dividend tax credit that require close examination before you make a decision. Let's look at the situation of a 75-year-old widowed grandmother who lives with her children in Ontario. She has a small pension, which, when added to her CPP and OAS payments, gives her taxable income of $25,000 a year. She has recently inherited a modest investment portfolio from her husband, which consists almost entirely of bank preferred shares. The dividends from the portfolio will add $3000 a year to her income.

In this case, there is no tax advantage to putting the preferred shares into a TFSA (assuming they will never generate a capital gain). That's because at her income level, the effect of the dividend tax credit will be to reduce the tax payable on the investment income to zero. (This would also be true if she lived in British Columbia, Saskatchewan, Manitoba, Nova Scotia, Prince Edward Island, or the Northwest Territories.)

Compare her situation to that of a Quebec-based senior vice-president of a large public corporation who owns 100,000 shares of the company's common stock. In his case, the dividends will be taxed at a rate of almost 30 percent. He should contribute $5000 worth of his shares to a TFSA every year and give his wife $5000 worth to do the same.

There is also another circumstance in which dividend-paying securities should be considered for TFSA accounts. That's when a taxpayer is vulnerable to the Old Age Security clawback. I'll explain this in more detail later in this chapter.

An Interest Strategy

Although interest income is taxed at your marginal rate, the tax-saving potential of a TFSA for GICs, Canada Savings Bonds (CSBs), and so forth is limited, especially at a time when rates are low. For example, if you invested $5000 in the S114 issue of CSBs, which came out in the fall of 2008, and the bonds earn 2 percent a year for the next five years, the total amount of tax-sheltered income you receive will be only $520.

However, many people prefer the safety of interest-bearing securities to the risk of stock market investing. For those who have a long time horizon, there is certainly an advantage in using a TFSA for this purpose instead of leaving the money in a taxable account. The key is to aim for the highest possible return, consistent with safety.

In the fall of 2008, for example, one major bank was offering four-year GICs with a yield of 4.5 percent. If TFSAs had been available then, you could have invested $5000 in the GIC and tax-sheltered the interest. At maturity, you would have earned $963 in tax-free profit.

Avoiding the Dreaded Clawback

One of the most contentious tax laws on the books is the clawback of Old Age Security payments from Canadians age 65 and older who are deemed to be in the "high-income" category. For the 2008 tax year, the threshold that pushed people into this class was net income exceeding $64,718 (the figure increases annually in line with inflation).

The tax is a stiff one: a 15 percent surcharge on every dollar of net income above the limit until the entire OAS payment has been recovered. For a Manitoba resident with taxable income of $70,000, the effect is to increase the marginal tax rate on the affected portion of her income to 54.4 percent.

Obviously, OAS recipients who are close to the threshold are motivated to do anything they can to stay below it. TFSAs provide two new ways to achieve this.

The first derives from the fact that TFSA withdrawals are not considered to be taxable income, unlike RRSP withdrawals or RRIF payments. This isn't a significant factor now, but as time goes on and TFSA balances increase, people who are close to the threshold will be able to draw cash from the plans without risking having their OAS payments clawed back.

The second way in which TFSAs can be used to reduce or eliminate exposure to the clawback is more subtle. It involves using the plans to circumvent what I regard as one of the most unfair aspects of the Income Tax Act, but one that no government seems willing to change.

We have already looked at the advantages of the dividend tax credit. But the credit can be a double-edged sword when it comes to the OAS clawback. That is because of the way it is calculated and the structure of the income tax return.

There is nothing simple about the dividend tax credit. Calculating it is a two-stage operation. The first involves a "gross-up" of the actual dividend income you receive to what is technically called the "taxable amount of dividends." The second step is to multiply that number by a percentage factor to arrive at the actual amount you can deduct from your income tax. For what the government classifies as "eligible dividends," which includes all public companies, that factor is 18.9655 percent. For dividends that are not deemed eligible (typically those from private companies), the factor is 13.3333 percent.[2] As I said, this is not simple!

Here is the problem as it relates to the clawback. The grossed-up amount of dividends received is used to calculate net income. (This is unlike the treatment accorded to capital gains, where only half the profit is included in the net income calculation.) The result is that people who receive dividends run the risk of incurring tax on money that they never actually received—I call it "phantom income."

It works like this. Every dollar of eligible dividend income you collect is grossed up by 45 percent. So for purposes of calculating exposure to the OAS clawback, $1.00 of income is treated as if you had actually received $1.45. Clearly, people who depend on dividends for a significant portion of their retirement income could find themselves pushed over the clawback threshold as a result.

This is not a theoretical exercise. Low interest rates and the demise of income trusts have forced many older people to look for other investments that will provide them with the cash flow they need to live on. As it happens, the big banks came out with new issues of high-yielding preferred shares in 2008 as a way to increase their capital base. These preferreds offered dividend yields of 5 percent and more, which would be equivalent to about 7.2 percent from a bond in after-tax terms.

The trap is the gross-up. Someone who receives $15,000 in eligible dividends will have to declare $21,750 as net income, which could be enough to move her into clawback territory.

You can use TFSAs to alleviate this dilemma. By using the plans to invest in preferred shares (or dividend-paying common stocks), you lose the dividend tax credit, but you also avoid the gross-up problem. This strategy isn't applicable to everyone, but it should be considered by those who have invested (or want to invest) in dividend-paying securities and who have income that brings them close to the OAS threshold.

Inheritance Shelters

The next 10 to 20 years will see an intergenerational transfer of billions of dollars in personal wealth. As the money passes from parents to children, the issue will become how to manage it in a tax-effective way.

Once an estate has been probated and all taxes paid, the remaining amount passes to the heirs tax-free. After that, if any portion of the money is invested, the profits are subject to tax at the applicable rates. Or at least that has been the case until now.

As time passes, TFSAs will provide an increasingly efficient way to shelter part or all of an inheritance from future taxes. By 2013, for example, a couple who has not made any TFSA investments will have $52,000 in available contribution room, as shown in the table on page 18 in Chapter 3. By 2018, this will have increased to $109,000.

Although this may not be enough to shelter the full amount of an inheritance from tax on the investment income, it will certainly help to reduce the bite. If the inheriting couple combines this approach with another tax-avoidance technique, such as paying off the mortgage on their tax-free principal residence, the proceeds from all but the largest estates may eventually end up being tax-exempt for as long as they live.

The same principle applies to lottery winnings, should you be so lucky.

Investment Loans

It's against the law to use an RRSP as collateral for a loan. That is not the case with a TFSA. The money in a TFSA can be used as security if you need to borrow cash for any reason. This loan can be for any purpose, from obtaining emergency funds to adding to your investments.

To illustrate, let's assume that you have accumulated $10,000 in a TFSA and invested the money in five-year GICs. Unless you have chosen redeemable GICs, that cash is locked in until maturity.

Suddenly, you are laid off and you need the money. You can't cash in the GICs, but you can go to the bank and ask them for a loan, using the assets of your TFSA as collateral. Since the money in the plan is in guaranteed certificates, there should be no problem obtaining the temporary cash you need.

Another possibility, and one that will probably be promoted by financial advisers during periods when stock markets are rising, is to use the money in a TFSA to leverage your investment portfolio. Because of the risks involved, this is not a strategy I recommend except for very knowledgeable investors, but if you know what you are doing it is a way to potentially increase profits. (It's also a way to increase losses, as people who had borrowed to invest learned to their dismay in the crash of 2008.)

To illustrate this situation, let's look five years down the road. You've been contributing the maximum amount to a TFSA every year and, with the earnings on the invested money, your plan has a value of $35,000. The entire amount is held in a diversified portfolio of mutual funds.

You decide to use the TFSA as collateral to borrow additional money to invest. Since the mutual funds are not guaranteed, the bank won't offer a loan equal to the full value of the plan, but it agrees to advance you $20,000 at prime. You invest the money in a non-registered portfolio of mutual funds, bringing the total amount of your assets to $55,000.

Over the next five years, your investments earn an average of 7 percent annually. Some of that return will be tax-sheltered by the TFSA, but the money earned on the non-registered portfolio will be taxable. At the end of that time, the original $35,000 in the TFSA will have increased to $49,089. Assuming an average tax rate of 25 percent on the non-registered portfolio, the $20,000 you invested there will be worth $25,831.

However, you need to subtract the interest cost of the loan from your return. As is the case with RRSP loans, you cannot deduct the interest expense on a TFSA loan for tax purposes, so you are on the hook for the full amount. For purposes of this illustration, let's assume the interest cost reduces your net after-tax profit by half. Your actual gain on the borrowed $20,000 after five years is $2,916.

(In their booklet on Tax-Free Savings Accounts, the Tax and Estate Planning team at Mackenzie Financial suggests that you can make the interest deductible by transferring assets from a non-registered portfolio to a TFSA. "Your non-registered assets could then be repurchased with borrowed funds," the team says. "In this case, a direct link from the borrowed money to an eligible non-registered investment would be established, and interest should be tax-deductible."[3])

At this point, you repay the bank loan and pocket the money. The end result is that you have completed the transaction with a total gain of just over $18,000. Since you only had $35,000 of your own money at risk (the rest came from the bank), your return on investment for the period is 51.4 percent. That works out to 8.65 percent annually. The bottom line is that you have improved your average annual compound rate of return (which was nominally 7 percent) by almost one-quarter through leveraging.

Of course, the higher the rate of return you earn, the greater the impact of leveraging. But the risk quotient also increases. This is why I stress again that only experienced investors should consider this strategy.

√Action Summary

1. Give careful thought to the securities you hold in your TFSA, with a view to maximizing tax effectiveness.
2. Be sure you understand the differences between the tax planning guidelines for RRSPs and RRIFs and those for TFSAs.

3. Focusing a TFSA on capital gains has the potential of producing large profits quickly, especially coming out of a bear market. Beware of the increased risk in this approach.
4. Do not automatically invest in dividend-paying stocks within a TFSA, especially those with little or no capital gains potential, such as preferred shares. Examine the tax implications carefully before deciding.
5. If you use a TFSA to hold interest-bearing securities such as bonds or GICs, look for the highest return consistent with safety.
6. The "gross-up" applied to dividends can result in some people who collect Old Age Security being pushed into an extremely high tax bracket on the basis of money they never actually received. Anyone in this position should consider putting dividend-paying stocks in a TFSA.
7. Use TFSAs as tax shelters for future investment earnings from inheritances.
8. TFSAs can be used as collateral for a loan, although the interest is not tax-deductible. If—and only if—you are experienced and knowledgeable, you can take advantage of this to increase the size of your investment portfolio through leveraging.

12

Yes, You *Can* Be a Millionaire!

TFSAs can make you a millionaire! Not in one year, or five, or even 10. But if you're young enough and stay with the plan, it is certainly an attainable goal. When you combine TFSAs with RRSPs, it's almost a sure thing, providing you can save enough and you invest wisely.

Of course, being a millionaire isn't what it used to be. Fifty years ago, a millionaire was someone who could live like royalty. These days, it's anyone who can afford to drive a car! Well, that's overstating the case, but many families who have mortgage-free homes and some savings put aside are probably getting close to millionaire status.

Nonetheless, the idea of being a millionaire remains a financial dream for many people. TFSAs will make that dream easier to achieve, but you will still need discipline and investment acumen to bring it all together.

In my book *6 Steps to $1 Million*, I wrote that there are two tracks to great wealth. One is to create it through hard work and innovation. The other is to save it. The new TFSAs are part of the savings track.

Let's look at four fictional couples and see how each might gain millionaire status with TFSAs and how quickly it could happen.

Sean and Alison: Slow and Steady

We'll begin by considering the situation of Sean and Alison, who live in Halifax. They are both 25 years old and were married last year. Alison inherited the family home after her mother died, so they are living mortgage-free. This enables them to save more than most young people their age.

Both of them had made RRSP contributions before the wedding and invested in mutual funds. They were shocked when they discovered that their retirement plans had lost 40 percent in the stock market meltdown of 2008. After that, they decided "never again." In the future, all their money would be put into safe securities such as GICs. They both understand this will reduce their potential returns, but that is a price they are willing to pay for peace of mind.

Both Sean and Alison opened TFSAs on January 2, 2009, and contributed the $5000 maximum. The money was invested in five-year GICs. They intend to continue doing this for the foreseeable future, increasing their contributions as the limits rise. Over the years, as interest rates rise and fall, they expect an average annual return of 5 percent.

How long do you think it will take them to accumulate a million dollars between them in their TFSAs at this slow but sure savings rate? Would you believe they will have reached that goal by the time they are 56 years old? That's right—assuming that inflation runs at 2 percent a year and contribution limits increase as per the existing law, even a low-risk investment program can make a young couple millionaires well before their normal retirement age.

This table shows their progress.

How Sean and Alison's TFSAs Grow

Years	Contribution limit (per person)	Period-end TFSA value
2009-2011	$5000	$33,101
2012-2016	$5500	$106,068
2017-2020	$6000	$183,233
2021-2024	$6500	$281,555
2025-2027	$7000	$372,276
2028-2031	$7500	$520,389
2032-2034	$8000	$655,377
2035-2037	$8500	$814,953
2038-2039	$9000	$937,230
2040	$9500	$1,004,042

Assumptions: Maximum contributions are made at start of year. Inflation rate is 2%. Average annual return is 5%.

Anil and Sujata: Buying Blue Chips

Anil and Sujata live in Regina. He is 43 and she is 42. They have two children, both of whom are now living away from home. They jointly run a successful hardware store. Their mortgage is paid off. However, the cost of raising a family and paying for their house has left them with no retirement savings. Now they want to remedy that.

Because they had no investments, they weren't hurt by the market collapses of 2002 and 2008. But many of their friends were. They don't want the same thing to happen to them, but they also realize that because they have no money put aside for retirement and have a relatively short time frame, they will have to take more risk if they are going to be able to sell the business and retire when Anil reaches 65.

Together, they decide that considering the circumstances the best strategy is to use their TFSAs to invest in a portfolio of blue-chip stocks. They realize that the markets will continue to fluctuate over the years, but they believe that by dollar-cost averaging their investments over a long period of time, they will be able to achieve an average annual compound rate of return of 8 percent, including dividends. Can they achieve their million-dollar objective by 2031? Let's take a look.

How Anil and Sujata's TFSAs Grow

Years	Contribution limit (per person)	Period-end TFSA value
2009–2011	$5000	$35,061
2012–2016	$5500	$121,212
2017–2020	$6000	$223,306
2021–2024	$6500	$367,071
2025–2027	$7000	$511,490
2028–2031	$7500	$768,875
2032–2034	$8000	$1,024,569

Assumptions: Maximum contributions are made at start of year. Inflation rate is 2%. Average annual return is 8%.

The answer is, not quite. Under these assumptions, their combined plans will be worth about $770,000 in 2031. But if they continue on the same course for another three years, when Anil will be 68, they'll achieve the million-dollar plateau.

Of course, if they save money in an RRSP as well, they'll reach a million dollars easily, and much sooner. If they each contribute $10,000 a year to an RRSP (assuming they have enough earned income to do so), their plans will be worth almost $990,000 after 20 years, again assuming 8 percent annual growth. Add that to the TFSAs, and they are well beyond the million-dollar mark. And here's the kicker: If their marginal tax rate is 35 percent, their RRSP contributions will generate tax refunds of $3500 each (or $7000 for the two of them), which will cover a large portion of the TFSA contributions. This is a good way to make both plans work in tandem.

David and Rebecca: Rolling the Dice

David is a stock broker and Rebecca is a chartered accountant. They are both very savvy about money and investing, and they are determined to get as rich as possible as quickly as they can. They understand the risk involved, but because they don't plan to have children, they are prepared to live with that. David is 32 and Rebecca is 30. They live in Montreal.

David knows all the tricks of the brokerage trade. He knows how to use options, how to leverage investments through exchange-traded funds, and how to play market cycles. He understands the investment rules governing TFSAs and is convinced he can operate within them to generate an average annual return of 15 percent on their money. A target this high is extremely aggressive and requires active management of the account and a lot of intestinal fortitude. David believes he can do it, and Rebecca supports him.

They decide they are going to push their TFSAs to the limit in their investment choices. He reviews the portfolios at least once a day, buying and selling regularly. He buys energy stocks when oil is cheap and sells when crude spikes higher. He trades in and out of gold shares. He buys exchange-traded funds that pay off double when the indexes they track move in the right direction.

Most of the time, it works. Like all investors, David suffers some setbacks along the way, but they are more than offset by years in which he is able to double the money in the plans. Over time, he achieves his 15 percent average annual goal. So let's see how much money they end up with.

How David and Rebecca's TFSAs Grow

Years	Contribution limit (per person)	Period-end TFSA value
2009-2011	$5000	$39,934
2012-2016	$5500	$165,612
2017-2020	$6000	$358,565
2021-2024	$6500	$701,784
2025-2027	$7000	$1,123,233
2028-2031	$7500	$2,050,677
2032-2034	$8000	$3,182,717
2035-2037	$8500	$4,908,402
2038-2039	$9000	$6,535,867

Assumptions: Maximum contributions are made at start of year. Inflation rate is 2%. Average annual return is 15%.

By the time David turns 50, their combined TFSAs have passed the million-dollar level, but he's just getting started. Compounding works like a snowball rolling downhill, rapidly increasing your savings in size as it goes. It only takes an additional four years or so to add another million to the pot. By the time he is 60 and Rebecca is 59, their TFSAs have accumulated almost $5 million, all tax-free. They'll be able to retire very comfortably on that money, although David will probably want to keep on going. He's the type you'll see in the library of a cruise ship, following the markets via satellite internet as he and Rebecca tour the world.

Jenny and Paul

Of course, many families will not be able to put aside enough money to make a maximum TFSA contribution. The budget is stretched thin just keeping up with household expenses; there's hardly anything left over at the end of the month.

Jenny and Paul are in that position. The 22-year-old Winnipeg couple is living common law for now, although they intend to marry within two years. They both work at modest-paying jobs, she as a library assistant and he as a trainee bus driver. They have no children but intend to start a family someday.

They like the idea of opening TFSAs, but they realize that they won't be able to contribute much, at least at the start. So they make a deal. They'll begin by putting $1000 a year each into their plans. Every five years, they'll add another $500 to the amount. They will invest the money in balanced mutual funds, which they hope will return an average of 7 percent annually. Here's what happens as the years pass.

How Jenny and Paul's TFSAs Grow

Years	Annual contribution (per person)	Period-end TFSA value
2009–2013	$1000	$12,307
2014–2018	$1500	$35,720

Years	Annual contribution (per person)	Period-end TFSA value
2019–2023	$2000	$74,713
2024–2028	$2500	$135,555
2029–2033	$3000	$227,043
2034–2038	$3500	$361,513
2039–2043	$4000	$566,267
2044–2048	$4500	$835,572
2049–2053	$5000	$1,233,466

Assumptions: Contributions are made at start of year. Inflation rate is 2%. Average annual return is 7%.

This one is an eye-opener! Even starting with very modest contributions and investing in moderate-risk balanced funds, Jenny and Paul are able to build their combined TFSAs to a value of more than a million dollars by the time they are 65 (the actual amount in the plans at the end of the year in which they celebrate their 65th birthdays will be $1,142,772.)

So even young people who don't have a lot of money can use these plans to create significant personal wealth if they are willing to make the commitment.

If you want to check out how TFSAs can work most effectively for your family, Scotiabank has created a useful online calculator that demonstrates how quickly your tax-free savings will grow. You can plug in any assumptions you wish, including initial lump sum contributions, monthly contributions, various rates of return, and time horizons. It's available at www.scotiabank.com/tfsatool.

A Tax-Free Future?

Tax-Free Savings Accounts were really created out of political expediency. As we saw in Chapter 1, Finance Minister Jim Flaherty had painted himself into a corner when it came to presenting his 2008 budget. Having given away everything that was left in the store in his Economic Statement the previous October, he badly needed something to showcase in February after the anticipated election failed to materialize. TFSAs fit the bill and the immediate cost to the Treasury was minimal.

As it turned out, no one gave the Conservatives much credit for TFSAs in the election campaign that took place in the fall of 2008; in fact, they were barely mentioned. But now they're here, and at some time in the future another finance minister may look back and ask, "Why?"

As the years pass, the amount of money invested in TFSAs will reach hundreds of billions of dollars. Some economists are already predicting that the time will come when many older Canadians will pay no taxes at all while at the same time drawing heavily on government programs such as OAS and medicare.

Whether this will be sustainable is something that future governments will have to decide. It is not inconceivable that at some point we may see a freeze on TFSA contributions or a tax on the withdrawal of investment earnings, albeit at a reduced rate.

But all of that is problematic, and if any changes are made to the system, it won't happen for many years. For now, Canadians have an extremely valuable new savings program with which to build their personal fortunes. Make the most of it!

Action Summary

1. Make your TFSA contributions at the start of each year to maximize tax-sheltered growth.
2. Decide on an investment strategy that suits your temperament and financial knowledge. Even a low-risk approach will enable a couple to accumulate a million dollars in their plans if they have enough time.
3. You don't have to be well-off to build wealth in a TFSA. Even if your income is modest, open an account and keep adding to it. Remember, the original reason why the C.D. Howe Institute promoted these plans was that they are an effective savings option for lower-income people. The younger you are when you start, the more effectively they'll work for you over time.

Notes

1: The Launch: Budget 2008

1. The Honourable James M. Flaherty, P.C., M.P., minister of finance, *The Budget Speech 2008*, Department of Finance Canada, February 26, 2008. Available at www.budget.gc.ca/2008/speech-discours/speech-discours-eng.asp.

2. Ibid.

3. Julie Smyth, "Budget Report Card," *National Post*, February 26, 2008. Available at http://network.nationalpost.com/np/blogs/posted/archive/2008/02/26/budget-report-card.aspx.

4. Benjamin Tal, "The New Tax-Free Savings Account: How Popular Will It Be?" *Consumer Watch Canada*, CIBC World Markets, September 11, 2008. Available at http://research.cibcwm.com/economic_public/download/cwcda-080911.pdf.

5. Steven Chase, "Small Change for Tighter Times," *The Globe and Mail*, February 27, 2008. Available at www.theglobeandmail.com/servlet/story/RTGAM.20080227.wbudget27/BNStory/budget2008/home.

6. Rob Carrick, "A Place to Park Cash But Not the Break They Promised," globeandmail.com, February 27, 2008.

2: A Little History

1. Department of Finance, *The Budget Plan 2004*, Annex 9. Available at www.fin.gc.ca/budget04/pdf/bp2004e.pdf.

2. "What Constrains Flaherty's Budget," *The Globe and Mail*, February 18, 2008. Available at www.theglobeandmail.com/servlet/story/RTGAM.20080218.wxebudget18/BNStory/specialComment.

3. William B.P. Robson and Finn Poschmann, *Steering through Turbulence: The Shadow Federal Budget for 2008*, C.D. Howe Institute, February 2008. Available at www.cdhowe.org/pdf/backgrounder_111.pdf.

4. Conservative Party of Canada, Platform 2004, *Demanding Better.* Available at www.theglobeandmail.com/bnfiles/politics/2004/Conplat form2004.pdf.

5. Conservative Party of Canada, Platform 2006, *Stand Up for Canada.* Available at www.scribd.com/doc/334166/Conservative-Party-of-Canada-Federal-Election-Platform-2006.

6. HM Revenue and Customs, *Explanatory Memorandum to the Individual Savings Account (Amendment) Regulations 2007.* Available at www.hmrc.gov.uk/SI/2007-2119-em.pdf.

7. Richard Shillington, *New Poverty Traps: Means Testing and Modest-Income Seniors,* C.D. Howe Institute, April 2003. Available at www.cdhowe.org/pdf/backgrounder_65.pdf.

8. Finn Poschmann and William B.P. Robson, *Saving's Grace: A Framework to Promote Financial Independence for Low-Income Canadians,* C.D. Howe Institute, November 2004. Available at www.cdhowe.org/pdf/backgrounder_86.pdf.

9. John Stapleton and Richard Shillington, *No Strings Attached: How the Tax-Free Savings Account Can Help Lower-Income Canadians Get Ahead,* C.D. Howe Institute, September 2008. Available at www.cdhowe.org/pdf/ebrief_64.pdf.

5: Saving for a Rainy Day

1. Statistics Canada, *The Daily,* September, 15, 2008. Available at www.statcan.ca/Daily/English/080915/d080915a.htm.

6: TFSAs or RRSPs?

1. Department of Finance Canada, *The Budget Plan 2008,* Annex 4. Available at www.budget.gc.ca/2008/plan/ann4a-eng.asp.

2. Pension Benefit Guaranty Corporation, www.pbgc.gov.

3. James Daw, "Teachers Take Pension Cutback," *Toronto Star,* October 1, 2008. Available at www.thestar.com/Business/article/509241.

4. Richard Shillington, *New Poverty Traps: Means Testing and Modest-Income Seniors,* C.D. Howe Institute, April 2003. Available at www.cdhowe.org/pdf/backgrounder_65.pdf.

7: Some Shelter for Seniors

1. Canada Revenue Agency, *2008 Interim Statistics (2006 Tax Year)*, Table 4. Available at www.cra-arc.gc.ca/gncy/stts/gb06/pst/ntrm/table4-eng.html.

2. Julie St-Arnaud, Marie P. Beaudet, and Patricia Tully, *Life Expectancy*, Health Reports, Vol. 17, No. 1, Statistics Canada, November 2005. Available at www.statcan.ca/english/studies/82-003/archive/2005/17-1-e.pdf.

8: TFSAs of RESPs?

1. A.J.C. King and W.K. Warren, *Transition to College: Perspectives of Secondary School Students*, Social Program Evaluation Group, Faculty of Education, Queen's University, 2006. Available at www.collegesontario.org/Client/CollegesOntario/Colleges_Ontario_LP4W_LND_WebStation.nsf/resources/School+-+College+Transition+-+Full/$file/CO_TRANSITION_COLLEGE_FULL.pdf.

9: A New Way to Split Income

1. Ernst & Young, 2008 Personal Tax Calculator, www.ey.com/GLOBAL/content.nsf/Canada/Tax_-_Calculators_-_2008_Personal_Tax.

2. Department of Finance Canada, *The Budget Plan 2008*, Annex 4. Available at www.budget.gc.ca/2008/plan/ann4a-eng.asp#personal.

3. Department of Finance Canada, Tax-Free Savings Account calculator. Available at www.budget.gc.ca/2008/mm/calc_e.html.

10: Leaving More for the Kids

1. Department of Finance Canada, *The Budget Plan 2008*, Annex 4. Available at www.budget.gc.ca/2008/plan/ann4a-eng.asp.

2. Department of Finance Canada, *Legislative Proposals and Explanatory Notes Relating to the Income Tax Act, the Excise Act, 2001 and the Excise Tax Act, July 2008*. Available at www.fin.gc.ca/drleg/bia2008e.pdf.

11: Tax-Saving Strategies

1. To illustrate, suppose you buy a mutual fund at $10 a unit and receive an ROC distribution of $0.40. Your ACB will be $9.60 ($10 – $0.40 = $9.60).

2. Rates as per 2009 tax year. In the 2008 budget, the federal government announced it will reduce the amount of the gross-up and the tax credit percentage in three stages from 2010 to 2012 to reflect reductions in the corporate tax rate.

3. Mackenzie Financial Corporation, Tax and Estate Planning Team, Tax-Free Savings Accounts (TFSAs), 2008.

Acknowledgments

No author can work in isolation. Every book requires extensive research and the help and co-operation of others. That was especially true in this case because Tax-Free Savings Accounts are so new that very few people have had an opportunity to study them and to come to grips with all their intricacies.

My first words of thanks are directed to the staff of the federal Department of Finance. They graciously fielded all my queries (and there were many of them) and followed up with the answers in time to meet my tight deadlines. The people in our public service don't get enough recognition for efforts such as this, so I'm taking this opportunity to say a heartfelt "thank you."

Next on my list is William B.P. Robson, president and CEO of the C.D. Howe Institute. The institute was the leading advocate for introducing Tax-Free Savings Accounts to Canada and published several research papers on the subject starting as far back as 2001. Robson, along with the institute's director of research, Finn Poschmann, took a leading role in bringing the need for these plans to the attention of the Canadian public. Their reports are quoted extensively in this book, and William Robson was kind enough to spend time providing me with additional background information on this complex subject.

Scotiabank was also extremely helpful in my research. They provided me with complete details of their in-depth TFSA survey, which contained some valuable insights into Canadians' views about, and reactions to, the program. I was also impressed by the online calculator Scotiabank produced to help people understand how TFSAs can be used most effectively.

My thanks also go out to the staff at the Ontario Ministry of Education, who helped to find elusive statistical information for the chapter on education savings. As well, I want to thank Sandy Cardy, vice-president of Tax and Estate Planning Services for Mackenzie Financial, for sharing some of the ideas her company has developed for how investors can best use these plans.

Perhaps the biggest contribution of all was made by my chief researcher (and daughter), Kim Pape-Green, who used her training as a library information technician to search the internet and the library system for all references to TFSAs, ISAs, Roth IRAs, and other facts that might be helpful to me in writing this book. Kim also prepared the endnotes and the index, operating (as we all were) under intense time pressure to meet the publishing deadlines.

Of course, this book would not have been possible without the support and encouragement of my long-time editor, Andrea Magyar, and her team at Penguin Group (Canada). Special thanks also to senior production editor Sandra Tooze and my copy editor, Heather Sangster.

As you can see, creating a book is really a massive team effort. All I had to do was to write the words.

For More Investment Information

Sleep-Easy Investing

Gordon Pape's best-selling book *Sleep-Easy Investing: Your Stress-Free Guide to Financial Success* is now available in a paperback edition from Penguin Group Canada.

Sleep-Easy Investing is a must-read in these turbulent times. In it, Gordon Pape offers a totally new approach to investing, one that will take the anxiety out of your financial decisions while still enabling you to earn good returns. He describes the philosophy outlined in the book as a "health trumps wealth" approach to sensible money management.

The book is filled with personal anecdotes, real-life emails from investors in trouble, and down-to-earth, practical advice on how to succeed without stress. "This book looks at investing from a human perspective rather than as an exercise in numbers," says Gordon Pape. "Over the years I have come to realize that financial experts sometimes forget that human psychology is the most important factor when it comes to investing success and personal health. I think this book will completely change the way many people feel about investing—for the better!"

Sleep-Easy Investing is available at bookstores across Canada.

Newsletters

Gordon Pape is the editor and publisher of several investment newsletters. They include:

Internet Wealth Builder. This weekly email newsletter covers all aspects of investing and money management, including stocks, bonds, mutual funds, income trusts, taxes, and general economic comment. The seasoned team of contributing editors includes some of Canada's best investment minds. The newsletter takes a conservative approach to money management and was among the first to warn of the drop in the Toronto Stock Exchange in a lead article published in mid-June 2008, just a few days after the TSX hit an all-time high.

The Income Investor. This twice-monthly newsletter focuses on income-generating securities with the goal of providing readers with above-average returns consistent with reasonable risk. At a time when interest rates are low and income trusts are being phased out of existence, the guidance provided by this letter is vital to anyone seeking steady cash flow from their investments.

Mutual Funds Update. Now in its 15th year of publication, this monthly newsletter continues to represent the gold standard in sound, sensible mutual funds advice. One of its most popular features is the Ideal Portfolios, which provide models for investors of all types, from ultra-conservative to growth-oriented.

For information on these newsletters, visit www.BuildingWealth.ca or call toll-free 1-888-287-8229.

Websites

More financial information from Gordon Pape can be found at the following websites.

www.BuildingWealth.ca offers free investment articles, a Q&A feature, valuable free budget and net worth spreadsheets, book excerpts, and more.

www.SleepEasyInvesting.com provides excerpts from the best-selling book and advice for those who want to take the stress out of money management.

www.TFSAbook.com contains more information about Tax-Free Savings Accounts and how to use them most effectively.

Index